WASHING LINE TO FRONTLINE, SURVIVING YOUR SOLDIER'S TOUR

Judith E. Bray

AuthorHouse™
1663 Liberty Drive, Suite 200
Bloomington, IN 47403
www.authorhouse.com
Phone: 1-800-839-8640

© *2008 Judith E. Bray. All rights reserved.*

No part of this book may be reproduced, stored in a retrieval system, or transmitted by any means without the written permission of the author.

First published by AuthorHouse 12/22/2008

ISBN: 978-1-4389-2712-1 (sc)

Printed in the United States of America
Bloomington, Indiana

This book is printed on acid-free paper.

Contents

A BIG HELLO	1
CASUAL GIRLFRIENDS AND BOYFRIENDS	5
THE START	7
COMMON EMOTIONAL TWISTS	11
THE DEPLOYMENT IS KNOWN	13
THE INITIAL THOUGHTS	17
THE TIME LEADING UP TO GOING	19
PREPARATIONS	25
A WILL TO BE WRITTEN	29
THE CONTACT PERSON	31
COMPASSIONATE LEAVE	33
THE LEAVING DAY	35
CONTACT ISN'T TOO BRILLIANT	41
LINES DOWN	45
SENDING A BLUEY/LETTER	47
ON HOLD	51
HOLD UPS WITH ALL MAIL	55
THE LETTER YOU WISHED YOU HADN'T SENT	57
READING MAIL WHEN YOU FEEL LOW	61
SENDING A PARCEL	63
WHAT PARCELS DO FOR YOUR SOLDIER	65
WHAT TO PUT IN MY PARCEL	67
WHAT YOU CAN'T SEND	77
CHRISTMAS PARCELS	79
A CHRISTMAS STORY	81
THEY DO HAVE THEIR OWN SHOP	83
PARCELS43 SUPPORTING OUR TROOPS	85
PHONE CALLS	89
CARE WITH PHONECALL CHAT	93
PHONING CUDDLES	95
USING YOUR COMPUTER	97
INSTANT MESSENGER	99
THE EBLUEY SITE	101
OTHER EBLUEY SITE USES	103
EBLUEY CHATBOARD	105

PARADIGM	109
THE HOME PAGE POSTAL BEARS	111
BOXHAPPY	113
THE FORCES RADIO STATION	115
FRIENDS DON'T UNDERSTAND ME	117
FILL UP YOUR TIME	121
SPRING CLEAN	133
I WANT TO LOOK A REAL BEAUTY FOR MY MAN	135
NIGHT TIME	139
EATING	143
DRINKING	145
ALCOHOL	147
ARE RELATIONSHIPS GOING DOWN HILL?	149
A SISTER'S VIEW OF THINGS	153
CHILDREN COPING	155
SHOULD I GET A PET?	163
EMOTIONS WHEN THEY ARE DUE TO ARRIVE	167
PICKING THEM UP AT THE AIRPORT	169
R&R TRULY BEGINS	171
R&R IS OVER	173
THE LAST AND FINAL COUNTDOWN	175
A SEXY BEDROOM	177
DECOMPRESSION	179
THE TOUR IS OVER. BACK IN THE U.K	181
THE MEDAL PARADE CEREMONY	183
A POETRY AND PRAYER SECTION COMPOSED AND SENT TO AND FROM LOVED ONES	185

A BIG HELLO

A very big hello from me to you with my huge smiles to match. Now lighten up, relax back in your armchair and read this like a friend.

I have written this to help everyone who is at home while their soldier is away. You will laugh, moan and cry. You have to try and make from all of the "positives" to be the biggest impact on this tour and surpass the negativity of it. The happier you are will make your soldier happier because it is catching. Select the bits relating to your predicament, which can be many. I have gathered together the troubles and ways of a lot of people although I had very few problems which for me was most definitely excellent.

Having an insight into how and why things happen, what to expect, how to do things and the emotional problems that envelop you is a large part of being able to cope with your battle at home. This is relevant whether you are a mum, dad, wife, husband, partner, sibling, any other family member or a friend. You will find this a very interesting self-help book that I have specially got together for you. If only I had such a book to guide me when my son first went off to war it would have made certain things so much better all round. But there wasn't one then. I had to learn the hard way with many bumps, as the majority of us have to tackle, even now. I was one of the mums who had some big problems mastered a touch easier than my friends. I was sure that each thing faced would phase me out completely during the tour. However, everyone has to learn lessons of one kind or another, day after day after day so that life makes more sense to you.

This book is a helping hand to get you through various problems and more problems that may or may not occur while your soldier is deployed. A means of getting you into the swing of things. A way of you making every bit of joy that comes your way into an enormous bonus. We all wish everything of the tour experience will run smoothly without any problems but when life is turned on its head that can't be guaranteed at all. Believe me, even you will get used to standing on your head rather a lot to match it. Being used to it is an awareness and not a solution. Everything possible is upside down and a total mess. Collectively none of your haywire feelings can be wiped out completely. Far from it. Obviously you wont get all the problems in the book but it covers a lot of the situations that can go awry. Many lovely things that also happen are included. There are suggestions as to how they may be managed just that little bit better. Be cheerful and bubble excitedly when you are able to. That is what you always have to do as much as you can. Strive for this aim of the positive to grab onto tightly. Knowledge is a huge step forward with countless steps to follow upon your very difficult journey through this unknown wild forest ahead and so the more you know then the better things can be.

The way "In" to the way "Out" will have you searching which includes scrambling around the wrong trees and even walking back on the same wrong route, also via new clear paths and old rough and rocky paths at times. A totally unfathomable puzzle that makes it seem that there is no proper way to forge ahead in a straight line. The direction is haphazard. A bit of the one step forward and two steps back. A maze lies out before you. It does have an exit that eventually you will find but not forgetting the place to rest and to have a breathing space in the middle. There is your first aim to get to that resting bench.

All of us find it easier or harder depending on which things stress us to different degrees the most. There can be very many "downs" all of the way to encounter. However, what may seem not such of a particular problem for you, is for another what could seem like a mountain and vice versa. I have compiled this using my own experiences and the "ups" and "downs" of so very many other people too. It is how to pull your socks up when things are not going too brilliantly. There are different ways to make things a little more positive on this rather negative trip. Keeping busy and filling up your time is an invaluable remedy. You can do it. You can be strong. Believe in yourself. Trust in yourself.

You are not alone even if it really does seem that you are. No type of normality can be reached, or so you think. You are feeling so separated from not only your soldier but also the ordinary life around you that dwindles until you feel you could be on your own with little support. If you think positively then grotty things can be handled better. Thousands of people are going through similar ghastly stresses that you are experiencing. It doesn't really help you knowing that because the number one person is you. At least the idea of not being the only individual stressing out can make you feel somewhat relieved in a minor way.

You may think you are a bit nutty at times and doubt yourself. Also the people around you on occasions cannot understand you very well at all. Equally you think they are rather stupid to not see your disruption so that they too are nutty. Exaggerated feelings are normal. The way you handle them can be a blessing. All the ways to fill up your time is a big solver to that. There are handy hints and tips for both practical and emotional purposes. Advice is here for trials and tribulations. There are rules for you to get to know and also other information on how to do things correctly. These you will get to know gradually. There are different ways for you to keep in contact with your soldier. Sending letters. How you can send love and hugs. How do you send a parcel? What to send and what not to send. Phoning. Using Messenger. Sending e-mails. Using e-blueys. The list goes on and on for you to pick from as needed. I am sure all of this must cover a great deal for your roller coaster ride. It has parts of how to cope with the children too. It has handy links you can use.

It all contains highs and lows so it isn't always going to be down. It's a mix of both. The way that you try to master it all will give a better peace of mind for you and at the same time will give the same peace of mind to your soldier. If you think positively then so will your soldier too. Confidence is like a big building block. You have many of those blocks to build.

Now stick your head in the pages and see what is what. Many things, that you never thought would be relevant to you, will amaze you.

There is a special poetry section at the back. It will intrigue you even if you were convinced that poetry wasn't your scene.

CASUAL GIRLFRIENDS AND BOYFRIENDS

Be cautious before you get on the Roller coaster. If you have no deep feelings of love, respect and trust between the both of you then you will not withstand this tough time. It won't be an easy ride at all for anyone therefore if you have none of those essential points then you will break up. Relationships relying on just lust will not stand a chance. That is one huge warning but so very true. I have seen many similar people of such twosomes crumble and split up totally, very fast indeed, if everything is depending only on sex because there will be none. Zilch. It is clearly apparent but it does hold an important factor. Therefore your main holding link has disappeared. Then where do you stand? You have no essentials to fall back on. Then off you pop to perhaps another direction. Excuse my bluntness but it's a fact. Lets not pretend on that score. The last thing our soldier wants during their deployment is a horrific "Flash in the pan" relationship problem concerning things that are flimsy and tentative from the start. The loss of having their love life suddenly disappear before their very eyes is painful to a huge degree. They have enough worries out there without them trying to cope with partnership ones that become thrown into the mix of it. If the soldier is sad then it means he/she doesn't have his/her mind on the job and that can make their safety zone rather unbalanced. Think very hard about it all if you are girlfriends and boyfriends who are with no permanency between you both.

The two of you have to be solidly together and as one total unit. Joined at the hip even when apart. Solidarity speaks volumes. It is the key to getting through. The position has to be substantial enough to work.

Any down parts that might happen with even good relationships throughout the tour can at least be rebuilt using all the other tethers and strengths at hand to get on an even keel once more despite the difficult stresses. Lust holds no such back up and that is where non-important matches fall apart. Now it is up to you to decide if you can make it through and I don't say that light-heartedly because stability has to be the main consideration. The question is, "Is it lust or love?" Having a boyfriend or girlfriend soldier may sound glamorous but in reality when push comes to shove it isn't at all. It isn't a time for you to be flippant and treat the relationship with no real care. Our soldiers need to be able to rely upon home to get them through their deployment. They do not want emotional girl or boyfriend problems to knock them back, dump them and jilt them as if it's nothing and has no basis. It's bloody hard work that only the strongest relationships can handle and hold in one piece. You have been well warned. Do not put one tiptoe on this roller coaster unless you are pretty sure that the bubble won't burst and cause some horrific incident. This is a war. It is not a game. It is a serious situation that shouldn't be taken lightly. Close down your friendship before your soldier leaves if it isn't strong. Only you can judge that.

THE START

Everything is normal and you are getting on with your everyday life. No real problems in the world. Your soldier will come home and you will sense from his look that there is something very wrong. The time has now come that you hoped would never come. Your loved one has to give you the news that his/her regiment is off to war in a matter of weeks. It makes no difference whoever you are that you will feel crushed to bits. Screwed up faces are pulled to register the information and tears fall. The down turned mouth. Those huge heaving sobs. Surely this can't happen to you. But the world has come to hit you in the face & will throw your understanding of this life now, upside down at the hearing of those words. It's unbelievable. You have never had such a vast and complicated trauma to confuse you with just a couple of sentences with the mention that there is a deployment. You have stepped onto that roller coaster joined by all families and friends of other troops who are involved. All of these people who are in the same boat as you are going to feel the way that you do. Even though you think that you are being so OTT, extreme highs, lows, and mood swings, it is always the same way for everyone. It is overwhelming and as if you are staring vaguely through a mist. You are definitely not going insane although you may question this time and time again.

I can only give you the written hugs and information from what I write but real hugs are what you will need along this journey for sure from your own family and friends. Their support and love will hopefully be there to lean and rely upon. This is to be your new "normality" for many months. Strange, scary and so unreal. You will cry. You will laugh and moan as each day passes. Some days are much better than others. This book is the good the bad and the confusing mix of both. I don't write this through rose coloured spectacles to hide the "not so good bits" from you. It is a book of truth. I haven't written this to alarm you but it all has to be faced. There are comparisons to be made as to the level of the nice and nasty.

These writings can broaden your awareness just a little bit. The key to all of this is to develop your understanding and learn how to look at things sensibly. Managing different types of problems takes a lot of working out to be anywhere near successful. This book is an outstretched helping hand to hold onto from the day you know deployment is just around the corner until the day they return at the end of their tour. This is for you to use and read repeatedly to remind you as the weeks move forward and you feel the odd need to take a glance to give you an idea on any particular subject that you are having difficulty managing. It is to help you make sense of things.

I have a son in the army and he has been to serve in Iraq twice so I know the effects that burrowed through me and other people who are left at home to struggle in the same way. Rank or the type of job they do or how many things that may differ from one soldier to another, are not at all relevant. They are an appendage but our emotions are deep within us. Our feelings are all the same to varying degrees, unless of course you are as tough as old army boots with no heart. How sad that must be for such a person who is without love or caring within them. Sensitivity is essential. If you are reading this then you will be full to overflowing with these essentials that are truly going to be needed. You want this book to make things as straightforward as possible for both of you while you plough through each day. Overflowing with concern in this way or that and struggling to make a silk purse from a sow's ear. The understanding will help to pull you through from start to finish despite every incident that springs out at you whenever it chooses. Your complicated life is only kind of normal and sometimes happy but with different things thrown in to it to make your life tilted and awkward. A threatening existence with a bit of confusion day after day makes it all rather stressful.

What I write is related to the army and I can only talk of that via my own and others experiences but the same emotions are relevant to all no matter which of the Forces the loved ones are from. I pray that these pointers will assist you in various ways even if your connection isn't in the army.

Try and smile whenever it's possible, even if they are just weak ones that you can muster. Smiles take fewer muscles whereas frowns take many which give you ugly wrinkles. You won't want to look in the mirror and not see your prettiness getting lost. Now you are embarking onto an awesome learning curve that wobbles unexpectedly and feels so unreal. A mix of things makes it possible to take an edge from your newly discovered mountain that with some very hard work can start to be reduced. Probably you can get it down to a smaller mountain. Fingers crossed.

COMMON EMOTIONAL TWISTS

We are only human and therefore we can't look at things in a cool way. Emotions pull you in every direction possible. They have no regularity at all so life is going to be swings and roundabouts and your life is going to be far from straight. Frightening feelings will be with you all of the time. Your imagination goes wild by waiting and wondering. Why has no mail arrived? What could have stopped it getting through? Why not a single phone call or e-mail? You knew it wouldn't be as regular as much as your heart would wish but sometimes it gets so o.t.t. that you cant stick all of this screwing up each day. You may think that something just has to be wrong. Why does everything feel so un-right? You know that "No news is good news" but this really does take the biscuit if you have heard nothing for many days or weeks. Your head is full of wild imaginings that are so way out and then you begin to doubt yourself. Every day your security blanket seems to be shrinking fast so that it seems it will have soon abandoned you.

No matter what your worry you end up running about like a headless chicken searching and searching all over the place to find out what could be the reason for the littlest of things that go minutely awry. Looking to see if there is any news you can dig up from somewhere on the TV, computer or by phoning friends to give you the answer.

Some days you will be jumped on by friends saying, " What do you think about such and such that is being mentioned on the latest news?" First of all you don't want to know that something has happened. You wish they hadn't said it because now its broken you to bits. Another reason to get you dashing about madly and at a loss in order to find out what has gone on. People will ask you where your soldier is based because an incident has happened at some place in the country your soldier is in. Could the trouble be where or near the specific camp of your soldier? Can it have been related with his/her regiment or camp? They mean well by trying to get involved and be interested in this situation of yours. They do really care even though at the time you won't see this at all. The way they have said it can appear to be rather cruel or harsh. It would seem they cannot gauge on what you want to hear and what you do not. A lot of the time it is because you are so touchy that everything gets blown out of proportion. You don't want to stick your head in the sand but this over powering additional information isn't really helping you manage in any kind of way. It isn't being a wimp by avoiding any news via the media. It is sensible to avoid it. It stops some of the stress and I actually didn't bury my head in the newspaper. Digging for information on many TV news channels is highly not recommended either. Don't over search for bad news on other sites or you will make yourself into a nervous wreck. Once you know of bad news that gives you the initial information then what is the point of reading or hearing it over & over again. You learn no more but just wash yourself with it and the result is a waste of time and breaks you up. Self-inflicted worry made by you. This is no time to develop ulcers. So do make a point by resisting that bad habit of immersing yourself repetitively for more information about it. It isn't an easy habit to break but give it a go to see if it helps. It can take a lot of will power to do it. Give yourself a gold sticky star if you do sort it out and ignore media. Then you will wonder why you ever became a newsaholic in the first place.

THE DEPLOYMENT IS KNOWN

On your marks, get set and here you go. Your soldier has to give you the news knowing it isn't going to be a simple thing to do. Giving any rather unpleasant news in life can be nasty at the thought of bringing up the subject let alone the actual doing of it. You are told the situation by your loved one. You both burst with intense pride and are so on a high with every fantastic event before you. But within a short time reality suddenly makes you see the whole picture. Your heart sinks. It is pounding so much you can feel it. It's as if you can hear it too. Thump, thump thumping away. You can't think too straight. You both have your heads spinning. What the hell is going on? Neither of you realise how it will be when so many hundreds of miles apart. Emotions grip you intensely. Every way you look you can't seem to find a clear space. Every nook and cranny round the room is filled with countless feelings of shock, horror and anger. The truth still doesn't sink in properly because you are numb. You feel drained. What is this? You can't take it in at all. Your mind realises that from now on you will be swamped with the unknown problems that stick out their nasty heads to effect you emotionally, practically and in many other ways that turns your normal and regular lifestyle ...the one that you know as normal... totally into an abnormal situation. It is too ghastly for you to visualise its enormity.

Both of you are ripped to bits. He/she might not seem to be quite so cut up about it and you wonder how this can be. That is because they love you and certainly don't want you to be more flustered than necessary. Equally you must help your soldier feel boosted up with many hugs, cuddles and sweet words. You both need to give each other morale boosters from now on. Perhaps the army tell them to do the softly softly approach to tell you. You will be in shock and your soldier is too but the men try to be macho so that their work mates don't rag them for seeming weak. He/she doesn't want to feel full of low self-esteem by letting his inner self down. The very gentle approach is so that you wont think they are incapable of doing the job before them. They want to show you strength and capability. They attempt to cover up their feelings. They may try and pretend that they are as unbothered and without stresses that you have. Big boys don't cry type of attitude. They are wrong because it takes a very brave man to outwardly weep. Tears are truth.

From the day they joined up they are taught very well to be immune and aloof to other emotional sectors as much as possible then, when tough things come along, it is part of their job to stay cool, calm and collected both outwardly and inwardly. A difficult thing for you to grasp but you must keep that in mind all through their tour. Your feelings are clearly open and stick out like a sore thumb whereas they have theirs partially hidden. Their emotions match yours even though you feel that you must be feeling the worst because you cant see their turmoil inside. A huge part of the training is to keep them safe. It is essential you remember that. Never get to thinking that they are not as stressed out as you are. Your feelings are strained because along with the shock you try to be as strong as possible. A very hard thing to do when torn in two.

My son doesn't live with me as he flew the nest many years ago. So my finding out was via the phone. He did the sweet gentle approach supposedly so he didn't have a gibbering wreck of a mother to talk to. Also he didn't want to fluster me. Constantly he was trying to cushion the blow. The call went on and on so that I got all the information as to dates, address etc. I wrote stuff down, but not before rooting around to find a biro that actually worked. He told me how he was feeling about the deployment and mixed in with lots of concern and our varied reactions between the two of us. Because we have such a close mum and son relationship we could discuss it freely. I kept telling him throughout as to how proud I was of him and that he would be in my thoughts every day. I told him that I would be worried about him. A silly thing to say really as that would go without saying. My mind wouldn't be completely straight until he returned home safe. He spoke so proudly and with such a gush. Actually he surprised me when he admitted he was rather keen with the idea of going to a different place outside of the UK to work. To him that was what it was. He sounded rather odd as if he was off on a holiday rather than off to war. At least that was how it seemed at the time as I listened to all he said. There was me biting my lip to stay in one piece. He said the idea of him being at work should be the way I looked at things too. I suppose it should be but it is so easy to say but not to do. He was going to find it unusual and dangerous. There was no doubt about that. It would be very dangerous indeed but also with a lot of interesting things to learn. War is nasty and we were both rather scared. Confidently he said, "Mum, we aren't always pointing a gun. We are not robots just there to fight with weapons." He assured me that he would be working knowing very well that as a soldier who has to go to war when needed that he would be with his mates doing the job expected of him. They would be working as a secure, well oiled and strong team with each watching out for the other. To have flaws in the way they do things, only brings weakness if they are haphazard. I nodded my head because it sounded a very good way to approach the whole thing but my head was then shaking "No" too as this didn't take into account the emotional turmoil that would destroy this very simplified description. General chitchat was mingled in with the usual stuff and the latest gossip talked about in normal phone chats so that we didn't just talk about his leaving or other army things. It was as ordinary as could be expected in such circumstances but that nasty news of him leaving left an extremely bitter taste in my mouth, which to me was most definitely very upsetting and mind-boggling. My head seemed to be of both good and all the not so good. Confused and shocked. I was frowning the greatest frown I had ever done. I was so very sad.

Towards the end of the call he asked me to keep in regular contact with his fiancé and little girl. The parting would crush them just like me. They would be so upset trying to handle this in their different ways. We would have to boost each other up. We would, without one doubt, have to be supportive with each other to somehow get through all of this. He asked if I would let other family members know. A very important thing to do. The moment he said it, I thought immediately that it would be a bit of a daunting task to tell them about this but when it came to it I found it actually was really quite easy. I suppose I was feeling rather at a low ebb to ever consider it to be anything but difficult. A little example as to how the imagination can bring negatives instead of positives when you are low.

There were lots of telephone hugs, cuddles and kisses but I was so deeply wishing they could be real ones. We had been chatting for ages but when I put down the phone reluctantly with many deep sighs, I still wished so very much that our chat had gone on longer. At once I puzzled as to whether I had said all the things I wanted to. I stared at my computer and reality struck me that I would be sitting there, sending and receiving many e's and having messenger chats on it with him from the other side of the world. It might be fun. It might be awful at times but who knows? A bit of both. Only time would tell. TIME, the importantly big word that will crop up for many things. Situation after situation.

Your fingers are going to use the keyboard lots if you have a computer. There will be a great many letters to write. So you see whether you are told of the tour face to face or via the phone, they are both emotional but different in intensity or type as to who you are as the family member or friend and how strongly, or not so strongly, you can cope in such a world. It's all a brand new experience that has to be faced in some way. Your way is the best. The way that seems most comfortable for you. Everyone devises his or her own comfort zone. That is your security blanket.

THE INITIAL THOUGHTS

For the weeks and days leading up to "THAT DATE" it might be a case of you putting on a brave face quite often. Attempting to do it at the very least. Tempers may flare up quite a lot with you wishing they had a different job like most of your friends. Why the heck can't he/she be the same as them? A 9-5 regular daily pattern. Always being able to come home after a day at work. Safe and sound every day for those other peoples lifestyles. Jealousy sneaks in there big time. However, if you are a spouse or partner, girl or boyfriend, you never considered his/her job when you fell in love. Cupids' arrow hit you both and that is what counts. Well doesn't it? The arrow didn't have a message on it about his/her career. Cupid cares not a jot about that side of things and that is how it should be. The whole person, and not the other things attached, is the most important of all. The attachments to any person are far from major when love brings you together.

For a parent it is very hard indeed to accept too that their son or daughter whom you brought up and nurtured with so much love and tenderness is now to be snatched away into such a horrible place. Into a country which is so far away from all the good things that had gone before them. Change. Such a big change. It is a weirdly strange and empty feeling of worry and more worry. Words to describe it are not possible. A person cannot explain an inner feeling for only that individual feels it. Your child who is now adult and cut the apron strings has the whole world upon his/her shoulders. This is so unreal. You must firmly take on board that it was the career he/she chose and wanted. At the time it all seemed fine. It is an excellent profession to be in. However, the tough side of it seems to make you consider that now the true reality it entailed never seemed to be any part of it. The probable dangers never occurred to you at the time he/she joined up. However, it is all included as part of the job. Something like this never truly entered your head before until this time when it actually opens your eyes while it unveils itself.

THE TIME LEADING UP TO GOING

For some people everything will go fairly smoothly without too many problems of erratic emotion and all seems to go through quite calmly indeed. Life doesn't seem to change much at all for those lucky ones.

The majority of people have some awful ordeal. It can be a very mixed up time. The soft hugs and kisses and so many ways of expressing your love, abound. There may even be more loving tenderness than before. Often, just when you go out, when you return or have had the best and happiest of days, suddenly without any warning, up come the variety of tempers and moods. Tears well up so much. Rows can happen more often because your soldier is gradually turning into the trained soldier mode before he/she leaves by just having the thoughts of what he/she is going to have to do once in the war zone. Aloofness and coldness may become a factor closer to the departure. Take that into consideration if you can. Phew, it isn't very easy to do and you probably wont consider it at all. How can you when the rows are rows with seemingly no particular excuses? Arguments happen to greater or lesser degrees from picking at each other or nagging or with vicious words that hurt as if you have been stuck with a knife or kicked in the stomach. There will be a great many fights from both of you in equal amounts. Biting your tongue doesn't seem to come into it. The rows balloon to immense proportions and who is going to stem its flow when it is so much easier to go with it and get stuck in. The claws are out and digging in deep. The mixed up feelings and the taking control seems totally impossible even though you are doing your very best to stay light and in some way happy. The effort to keep cool can be tough. What a pain in the butt that is and your loved one hasn't even left yet. Never stick yourself within four walls. Go out as much as you can together and enjoy things that will cut down on all the negatives that are happening. Do as many things that you always love to do. If you can go and visit other family or friends, if it's at all possible, can be a big help. This will give you masses of support to keep things looking brighter with their involvement and amazing times with them to really give you both a very positive boost. If you can't go and see them have a really long phone call where you can have a share in the chat. Try to arrange with them to be regular contacts to phone you and get you through. You must help each other to "Pick yourself up, brush yourself down and start all over again" Persuade them to also write to your soldier and I am sure they will be very pleased that you asked them to be a big part of his/her morale boost while in such a place where family and home is so important. The more letters the merrier. This will keep him/her less homesick. Throughout they will be shoulders to cry on and vice versa because it isn't only you who will be worrying and having a tough time. They will have their worries too.

A war is in the offing but until then there is this battle at home between you. A battle that will continue until the tour is over. Interrupting your ordinary life may contain a lot of sniffles and crying that both of you will try to hide from the other. Even if you are in the same room you will do your very best to hide any tears behind a hand or a newspaper strategically placed or by edging your chair just a little further back so those droplets are not spotted so easily. Perhaps a hasty move to another room to be extra sure might be more appropriate at times if full floods grab you. Oh how you want to make everything look smooth and as if you haven't a care in the world. You are both going through exactly the same muddles and doubts. Your mind is working overtime. You will find that lots of cuddles while chatting things through will help to reduce the tears or intensity.

Sometimes there will be rows of blame and feelings of guilt. Why the hell did you join up? If you loved me then you shouldn't want me to be left in a lonely hell. Why was I such an idiot to get involved with you in the first place? Military is no easy option. You will have to dig for every ounce of strength that you can muster.

Were you so naïve to not even have the thought about something like this happening because after all aren't rotten things meant to happen to others and not to you? Why you? Things could be said to you of a similar nature by a few of your friends and from now until the end of the tour. They can be angry that you ever put yourself in such a position. Be prepared for it. Also people who are against war may also point their finger at you. They will clearly have their say. It is tough coping with these attitudes, as certain people have no true understanding of it. This is when you have to be protective and supportive of each other through thick and thin 100%. You can do without all of these junk views to add to your plate of worries. Now is the time to try and close your ears from all this outrageous hassle that you find and is occasionally flying your way and try to deal with it as best as you can. It might come from all quarters. From people you never imagined would be so unsupportive. It wont be at all easy but if it happens then don't dwell upon certain peoples ignorance. Even parents have to face the barrage of comments by people asking why they let them join up in the first place. For example, "Didn't your son care if it meant you would have such worry due to his career?" How stupid some people can be asking such silly questions. Freedom of choice is what it is. We can't and shouldn't control the choices made for a future chosen by a son or daughter. I would never have even thought about such a thing until the comments were pointed my way. Oh well, you may have to face such judgmental remarks and dismiss them rapidly. Your soldier is putting his life on the line to protect and save everyone in the UK and these include the people who don't agree with our military. This is to make us secure and to give us all freedom. Our troops will be as proud of themselves as we are as immensely proud of them. Stick your chest out with your head held high. This is going to be a challenge but you will overcome it.

You have seen so many news items on the television showing all the yucky stuff and you think omg that is what he/she will be going to be a part of. You may hear that proper uniform for safety and other equipment, weapons and vehicles are not as good as it should be. Right down to the boots that they wear. There is a lot of flak about their food. You have to admit that such talk will make you angry and heartbroken with your soldier to be stuck right in the middle of it. The media are very quick to state all the doom and gloom. How can you get your head around that? You want things to be up to scratch for when he/she goes out there. Heavens, how will he/she survive all of this? Another reason to burst into tears. To help you I suggest you channel hop the moment the news comes on the TV, as this could be a more calming influence to assist you somehow if it isn't always taking over your life. It helped me. Too many times they put on film clips showing soldiers on patrol in the streets and the dangers there. Coffins with their bearers are shown. Another tearjerker for you to suffer. The tiniest thing will make you sob uncontrollably though most of the time when you cry there seems to be no apparent reason for it. It just happens at any time, any place and anywhere. This crying does release your inner bottled up thoughts so it can be beneficial. So as the tour presses on then it makes things easier for yourself and less distressing. If at any time you come to the conclusion that certain things seem to upset you for definite then you must try to avoid them at all costs.

The media wave their flags when it comes to flooding news of the not so brilliant side of things just so they get a good story. Media can be pretty harsh and thoughtless a great deal of the time so its best if you take it all with a pinch of salt. They can exaggerate all types of things and often get wrong information and twist it. There are discussion programmes on TV and the radio and information in newspapers as to the reasons why the army went to war in the first place or where numbers of soldiers will be moved to etc but in this book there are no such statements or political views regarding those. Don't fudge your brain up with such things.

It isn't all bad because at the same time immense pride runs through your veins knowing that he/she is somebody exceptionally special doing a vital job for the whole of the UK and other countries around the world. All your friends and family who you tell will ooze and burst with pride too. Many hugs & kisses from them to you both will go back and forth to boost you up. They surround you with their support and love. Admit it that you have probably told all and sundry about the going on tour bit. Pride exudes from you tons. Pride, pride and buckets of more pride. You will boast and brag about it. Too right that you brag big time.

The media can at times be a blessing as you might even consider telling your local newspaper to give it a big mention of how the difficult departure will affect your life and what it will turn into when your soldier goes to a war zone. Talk of the ways you can contact but the harshness of managing alone and trying to battle on as the best that you can. Say how all who are like you need support to keep you boosted up. If you do go to the paper then be advised not to make it politically based should you decide to do this. By putting in such a heartfelt article could be a reminding jolt to folks of our suffering as well. The battle at home is so rarely mentioned so aim it particularly towards information with your problems to be faced for such a huge chunk of time. You wave your flag as much as you can. Get your view shown to as many people as possible. Not enough people realise our problems. They don't see both sides of the coin. By doing this you can be a huge help.

PREPARATIONS

A lot has to be done. Just thinking about it is awesome enough. The preparation for the leaving seems an impossible task. You wonder in which order to sort it out. One can be so confused to know which is a priority so it is best to try and write a list and go through it and tick each item off as each one has been done. There is no priority as you will soon find out and the very long list you have written stares up at you. It all has to be completed satisfactorily and the lack of "TIME" to do it in can give such an uncertainty but dread the thought that you can't complete it. Bills need to be sorted out. It is probably a good idea to arrange with your bank to pay bills by Direct Debit or something similar so that will cut out a great deal of the pressure and give you certainty that essential payments are automatically seen to. It will save you having to have your head wondering if you are paid up on bills. Perhaps getting an off-road car license if the car isn't needed. Telephone the DVLA at 0870 240 0010 to organise it. The cancelling of any services that won't be used must be considered too. By doing this means no wasted payments. Every penny saved along the way is vital.

How will you cope with all the things that once done by him/her are now to be done by you and you alone? Get a chain fixed on the door. It is a simple thing to do that will be a great benefit to lessen your nervousness. Get into the habit of locking your doors and windows especially at night. Safety is paramount as you are the only strength when it comes to being careful. Not only will it give you a guarantee of relief but make him/her feel more at ease by being assured that you wont be an unreliable dilly! Put a helpful list of important telephone numbers that you might need to use. Important numbers of the Welfare Officer etc. that you may need at some point. They should all be put together next to the telephone or in another handy place so that they wont get lost.

You will be asked.

Do you know how to pay the vital electricity bills and others etc?

Please don't forget to pay them so that the electricity, gas or phone never gets cut off.

Have you got the plumbers number?

That should be known in case you end up with a flood. These things do happen so it is best to have a number "just in case".

What about the heating engineers?

Tons of questions of "Do you know how?" or asked by you "How do I do this that and the other?" You assume there will be no problems but really how will you manage if there are hiccups along the way? It is so over facing. You need to be very sure that you know how to do all this stuff of such importance to a certain degree. This is going to be a proverbial cushion to fall upon. All things go running through your mind. Eyes standing out on stalks with you trying to give the impression that it will be no trouble…NOT! Easy peasy. How you wish! Can all of this be simple for you as you are no mindless Dumbo. You assure each other that it will all run without a hitch. Smooth as a baby's bottom. A big lie of exaggeration there but so what. It sounds appropriate. At least that might put one worry off your minds if you both feel confident that all will run like clockwork.

There will be bantering back and forth as your heads whir through initial stupidly disturbing thoughts and doubts. You and him/her will talk the same things over and over again. So many various situations that could happen. So many queries that make ideas, not at all substantiated, spin around in your brain. The types of questions that you wouldn't know were inside you at all

Will I be missed and by how much or even forgotten about?

If only you knew how much because I will miss you and never in a million years will you be forgotten. How could I ever forget you!

Will the love fade away for some unknown reason?

Why ever should it fade away?

Thoughts of each other will be uppermost.

A strong attitude strengthened with love will keep it altogether in one solid piece.

Will we keep in touch often enough to keep our love alive?

We will write, e, messenger or phone each other whenever we can. Parcels will be a part of the home flying across to reach the camp. When we cant have such contact then the happy vibes will blend together to fill up that very important hole of sorrow.

Will the kids think their Daddy/Mummy has deserted them?

Everything will be told to them at their level of understanding to let them know the reason why a parent can't be at home.

It should be discussed with them together before the leaving. To always explain it as often as they need to be told can be good so they will never ever feel they have been deserted at any stage.

Will you find someone else while I am gone so long?

Never. Don't let that ever wander through your thoughts.

Both trust and love between each other is so very much and so strong that there should be no doubting on that score.

There will be no differences only a different way of showing it so there won't be any reason to find another person during this time of separation.

There will be ways learnt to keep your feelings alive.

Will I come back home?

How dare you talk like that?

Positive thinking is the only way to be. Negatives are not at all fitting. Neither will want to give off or think negatives.

There is very little chance of no safe return. Statistics say that it is much more likely to get run over, injured or killed by a car crash here than being killed in a war zone.

Most replies will be NEVER or DON'T TALK LIKE THAT or HOW CAN YOU THINK THERE WILL BE ANY DIFFERENCES. Things along those kinds of lines are bound to happen.

That's just examples to name only a few. The questions seem so endless and repeated many times but I am sure you get the gist of things with the ideas that buzz into your mind. Such muddles have to be straightened out somehow.

A great deal of support has to be strong in order to give you a leg up the ladder as the tour goes along.

A WILL TO BE WRITTEN

Every person going to a war zone has to make a Will for his or her next of kin or appropriate person. For some it is so unsavoury with the thought of that. Oh my! Doesn't that make you draw in a deep breath? You may be taken aback a little. Scratching your head and wondering what else will you be told next? A Will at such a young age is mainly why you are shocked. Don't be upset or let it stress you. Look at it as an official paper with no serious undertones for it.

The making of it doesn't always seem to bode well in your thoughts. Wills are not just for oldies. They are for people of any age even if you may not think so. It doesn't seem to ring true though. That really comes as a total surprise. It is probable that it never occurred to you in the slightest. Be calm about it. It is one of those additional things to add to your learning curve. This Will is vital and sensible. Try to see the benefit for lots of situations that may occur. Discuss it thoroughly. My son has written a Will quite a few times but it never seemed to bother me at all or him. However if you find it a bit curious and a jolt to the system then know that it is also the way it makes other people react too. You are not the only one to be rather shocked. It's a weird thing to get to grips with but soon it is just one of those necessary steps of no lasting concern for you.

THE CONTACT PERSON

He/she has to give a "Contact" name of next of kin or their particular choice, should anything go wrong. Health reasons, injury or, dread it should ever happen, death are all possibilities to be covered. I was the Contact person for my son. This is so there is a fast way to tell you any news. If you are not the next of kin or the chosen Contact then it may be very beneficial to find out who is and for you both to be supportive to each other and ask them to give you any important news that comes their way. Be on good terms with them so that they will be eager to let you know with haste. Similarly you can tell them when your soldier has phoned or written etc.

No information will be given to anyone but the Contact person even if you phone authorities to glean stuff. You could be anyone so strict rules have to apply.

The saying No News is Good News is very true. The only time you will hear news of a problem relating to your soldier will be by officials. That knock on the door that you never want to get. If you hear or guess any rumours then 99% of the time then that is all they will be with absolutely no basis. If you see sad or shocking news on the TV then be assured that the appropriate contacts have already been told by then. The Contact has to give permission to allow if any names can be given to the media. The family may want to tell other loved ones first rather than them finding out by a news broadcast. The army reaches the Contacts approximately 2 hours after any incident. So no news given to you means all is fine. The military don't hold back in responding with such information. It is as immediate as possible.

Anything in the media of a scary or sickening incident is going to rip up your emotions to unbelievable heights. Your heart goes out to friends & families of dead or injured. I cannot describe the awful feelings that kick in, as we are all different. You are so deeply upset. There is no way to stop these emotions because it takes as long as it takes. You will overcome it as soon as you can. People vary with the length in this time frame. All the troops will be at an all time low so we must grab the bull by the horns. We must focus on our Battle At Home to be ready to try and boost up our loved ones and bring up their morale as speedily as you can. Our task is very difficult but gather every ounce of your strength for the NOW and the future. We must handle it in some way.

If at any point Contacts are going away from home for a week or more or going on a holiday then it is best to inform the army so that they can get hold of them at a different phone number while they are gone. Telling your local police station is a good idea too so that they have your alternative number. Also it is best if you can tell your neighbours if you are going to be away. To be the Contact person is very important and it is essential that you are gettable at all times.

It's all a part of the sensible rules. You will find many such rules will be needed throughout the tour to cover allsorts of things. You will soon discover that. Wow, how complex this learning curve that you are now upon seems to be growing by the day. New situations can be absolutely mind blowing for you. You never thought about so many twists and turns that would be created or exist for very good reasons.

If for some reason your soldier needs to know of something major here that has happened which they should know of fast then contact the Army Welfare Officer at his/her camp here. That is your first port of call. Alternatively phone Army Welfare Information Service.... 01772 436569. They will get the details to your soldier in an hour so he/she will phone you back asap. That way there is no delay.

COMPASSIONATE LEAVE

Soldiers are allowed to come home for a short time (usually up to 2 weeks) if something untoward or serious happens with direct relatives. It isn't for Aunts or Uncles or friends. It is for a parent, wife, husband, children or siblings. The Contact person is the one to inform of the situation that they are needed home. The Army will decide on the amount of time they can be away. The requests may sometimes be disapproved of, so there is no cut and dried rules to this. Each decision is unique due to circumstances. The Army does have a huge heart because they want the troops to be as much at ease as possible in serious family situations. The utmost will be done to try to make a final and fair decision as to there being a valid reason for Compassionate Leave. This could be for a dangerous or critical illness when it is essential they visit home. It could be for a funeral. There are other reasons for Compassionate Leave so there can be many variations as to whether it is necessary.

They may be about to be a Dad so they are usually allowed home for the birth. At this time they get 2 weeks leave. However, even first births cannot always be guaranteed leave permission for it. It is up to the regiment to decide. They really do their very best to make it possible. The same rules apply for further births although they may take into account if other family or friends are available to be supportive to the mother-to-be.

Another deciding factor is the operational environment in which case if the soldier can or cannot be spared. Also it depends if they can safely be flown out. At such times they may not be allowed home. Not brilliant to have to be faced with a negative.

Anything with a specific date like a wedding to go to would have to be previously arranged well in advance. It is doubtful if this would be granted without great debate so you may miss it. Do also realise that all of the reasons are only for immediate next of kin.

Sometimes it is more appropriate for a soldier to have regular phone calls both in and out rather than Compassionate leave home.

The Joint Casualty and compassionate Centre (JCCC) Innsworth, Gloucester, GL3 1HW +44 (0) 1452 519951. This number is manned 24 hours a day, including weekends and Bank holidays. For further information on Welfare and Community Support Services available to Service families, see the following websites: www.army.mod.uk/servingsoldier/ rncom.mod.uk / rafcom.co.uk

A THOUGHT FOR EVERY DAY

"WE ALL LIVE UNDER THE SAME SKY BUT WE WILL BE SEEING DIFFERENT HORIZONS."

Look up at the moon, stars, sun and clouds so that you feel much closer to your loved one. He/she can see all that you see when he/she looks up which is a lovely way to think of things.

THE LEAVING DAY

What a hellish day this is. A boiling mish mash of emotions with terrific weight. You try to be all sweetness and light with glued on smiles to perhaps make each other believe things are ace and worry free. Things seem to be a lot of downs at the moment but wait and see. There are lots of things en route to make you smile, have fun and laugh about as each day passes. All the "ups" will be gathered to counteract the "downs". So far you have worked hard. Slogging your guts out and learning is difficult and over facing which after a while will get a bit easier to cope with and then you could as an afterthought wonder what all the extreme going away fuss at the leaving was all about instead of just pure and simple fuss. Ha ha, if fuss can ever be called simple!

That is the unfortunate way to say cheerio but for most it is no problem at all without any upset or bother. Being very confidant and all the kisses and hugs not having to be forced to happen will be easy as pie. So either way it can be. It all depends upon your ability to take the situation. If its hard for you or not is the difference at this point between yourself and someone else. Never compare yourself to another person in the same position as you. It can swing in either direction. You are unique.

Oh, how you perhaps wish it were a nightmare that you could awake from. Try as you might it isn't one. This is the real world. So many sloppy wet kisses, hugs and tears streaming down the cheeks as you cling on to each other as if you are stuck with super glue. Comforting words to brighten you both. You are in a total tizzy with repeated last minute thoughts checking and questioning that all has been done and everything needed has been packed. But the eventual departure happens. It is so overwhelming that you are unsure what to talk about without causing any fluster. Tears cannot be held back totally. If you don't cry outwardly then you will be inwardly feeling the strain. Reality is knocking at your door. It's Cheerio time. It's time for your final "Cheerio's". No, no, no because it all feels so wrong and unjustifiable. It is so distressing. Then you are suddenly alone. The time has come to set in your mind permanently that NO NEWS IS GOOD NEWS. If you hear nothing from officials then it means all is well.

From now on this is when, as if by a click of the fingers, the clock seems to slow right down from the fast way it has been from the start when it seemed all of a rush to get things done. TIME seems to run so much slower than it should so that it drags its feet. It will be that way for the duration. What is only ten minutes will seem like an hour. It becomes unbelievably in a "snail speed" slow motion.

You know the time the flight leaves so you keep looking at the clock. Staring at it so many times awaiting the flight schedule. Pacing up and down. Fidgeting. Making endless cups of tea and smoking like a chimney. Snacking and more snacking. That darned clock must have something wrong with it. It may help you to have a special friend with you for a shoulder to cry on and give you a bit more strength. Tears can be so frequent that many tissues should be at hand. I am sure the tissue companies are making a bomb at our expense!!!! Your voice might come out in a strange way so you sound like an idiot as well as look a disorderly unkempt mess. Far from pretty. A tiny hint for you to consider is if you wear make-up do not wear too much mascara on this day unless you like black streaks or smudges.

Once the clock watching started awaiting my sons take off was when it affected me then drinking fruit juice, being restless and being very irritable. Filling the ashtray with fag ends. Very charming..Not.

Fortunately I don't wear much make-up so I didn't have a problem on that score of it becoming a disaster. I am not the sort of person who cries outwardly. Not a tear ran down my face as all my tears were choking me inside. I still needed the box of tissues by my side, as my nose seemed to run rather profusely then got bunged up. I thought it would never stop.

My stomach churned over and over to the point I was feeling miserable and lost. It isn't any help being a person who doesn't cry as it meant all my feelings got bottled up. Not a good thing. I smiled false smiles in the hope that somehow I would look more normal to my husband...Yes, I think I over did that somewhat. My voice occasionally came out at various and different levels to the usual way so that it was out of control for sure. I wasn't at all convincing even with me doing my utmost to look unworried and unaffected by the whole thing. Why couldn't I be all cool, calm and collected like my husband? I questioned and questioned this. When I spoke to him I was far from coherent and he gave me an awesome look of disapproval. The look one gets from a schoolteacher who peers down their nose with piercing eyes at you because your work in class is rather poor and they scare you to death. Being over awed by such a " controlling schoolteacher" type of glaring experience. Just like that. Hard and very cheesed off glares came in my direction with lots of tutting. I couldn't help behaving the way I was even if I did seem occasionally unattached to the real world. I most certainly couldn't think as usual with my brain a bit different from the norm.

I wondered what my son would think if he knew how badly his Mum was taking it all. He has been to several war zones and although I got to know more information from experience, the emotional side doesn't get a great deal better with very little improvement in handling it all. Not one iota for some. Emotions are always as high each time. I think his Iraqi and Irish tours were the worst because they were constantly in the news. Nearly every night on the TV or daily in the newspaper where it was telling of some miserable happenings of which I didn't want to be told. Difficult to dodge totally. The media throwing the worst news at me over and over again. So often hitting me where it hurts and each time thoughts got into overdrive. Another very sharp and upsetting reminder to me. Channel hopping was a neat way to avoid it somewhat.

Tick, tick, tick as the clock goes on and on until the big moment. There must be something very wrong with the clock as time is taking an age by dragging so much. Eventually the take off time arrives. Imagination buzzes through a choc-o-block mind while you try to visualise exactly what it is like for him/her waiting at the airport before he/she boarded and what it's like now that he/she is on the plane and the things at that moment he/she would be doing and thinking.

You can explode with the same doubts and wonders repeatedly. Checking into your over filled memory bank. Have they taken or sorted out everything they should? Did they forget to pack something important? Why didn't I say this or that to him/her so he/she knew I love him/her to bits? Why couldn't I have held myself together for him/her in the weeks running up to this moment? Why did we have that row just before he/she left? Bucketsful of "WHY".

You may even consider writing a letter already but heaven knows what you will write. He/she has only just taken off. Will you even manage to see the page straight through those tears? You could make the paper wet if you cant pull yourself together as lots of crying doesn't help. In fact all you write then could be a downer so I suggest you drop that idea unless you are truly sure it can be something to boost their morale. Write if it makes you feel better to get your feelings off your chest but don't post it until you have re read it the following day. You can reconsider if it is a written immediate knee jerk reaction that should not have been something to greet him/her as their first piece of mail. You could regret sending something so involved with sadness. It is highly likely it will be a load of over emotional rubbish only fit for the bin. He/she does not want to have the first letter etc being a downer because he/she needs a terrific boost to feel sure you are managing everything very well.

This first day of weirdness may take you by surprise. Heck are you really going to be this way always? Mmmn possibly but not as sharp. It is most likely and probable and quite a lot of the time that it will catch you off your guard. It depends on the sort of person you are as to the difficulty and problematic heights it reaches. Positive thinking is going to be your saviour to minimise the "downs" that will surely turn up. Excuse the cliché.

The roller coaster, which is so much worse than any funfair ride, has started on its journey and you have been sitting on it since the day you were told of the tour, waiting for it to roll. When you get off it is so far away you can't visualise it at this point. The ghastly sickening ups and downs are ahead. That is all you can see at the moment. But hey there are many more ups than you think. Honestly. Even just little shaky type of smiles or huge grins at various stages can be found. You will get through this journey. You are closer to the return than it was, be it only a few hours. The way to count the time is to know you are always a nearer day or sleep. A nearer week or month. Think as brightly as you are able. Some people like to have a calendar to cross off daily or by weekends. Others prefer to hold the dates in their heads so that it isn't so evident or visible so often. You will make a choice that you find works best for you. I chose the dates in my head routine.

You might find it fun to make your own calendar or if you have kids then they may enjoy making one with you. A special Chuff Chart diary/calendar of large "write in bubbles" for each day of the tour with each bubble to be coloured and written in daily by you or the children once each evening comes. Attach photos to it. Make an edible one with a jar of sweets for 1 to be eaten and then watch the jar empty. You need resilience to do the edible one. For children Chuff Charts give them some idea of time as it passes. It isn't always an easy thing for a child to grasp in their little minds the very immense journey laid before them. It's hard enough for us to get a grip of the length of it all. So a Chuff Chart is an excellent way to show the bridge of time a little better for you.

My opinion was that looking at a calendar could be depressing for me. As for an edible Chuff Chart then I would need a cupboard full of packets of sweets, as I would be eating a bag of sweets per day instead of just one jellybaby/smartie/malteser or your particular sweet that you want to use. Others find it exhilarating and comforting. In everything there is no right or wrong choice in coping. Just do your own thing. You will quickly work out the way that in all things suit you the best. Individual choices that you find will click just right. Your method is the right method. Remember that.

The next important clock-watch is when the time comes for the approximate touchdown. Since the time they flew out you can find that you haven't been able to relax and sit down. Pacing up and down so much that it's a miracle a worn track on the carpet hasn't appeared. Time really is dragging its feet so very much and it is so obvious. Your mind is in hyper mode and it wont stop. Your box of tissues is by your side. Chomping at snacks and chocolate. Any diet you were on has seriously gone out of the window. Off goes your imagination once again as to how he/she is. How did the flight go etc? Phoning friends and family to chew over all the worries can help. Reassuring each other where at all possible to feel lighter.

The Eagle has landed. Where abouts will they be now? Your brain is abuzz with questions & imagination of things you don't really have any inkling about. The ideas choke you with the "not knowing". Even if it's at some unearthly hour you probably will be awake for it because you may have not been able to get to sleep very easily with your head so wound up with extra brain activity. Tossing and turning with no solace. The house seems so quiet & so empty. A pin could drop and you would hear it. An unfriendly atmosphere surrounds you. The loneliness and silence grabbed you the moment he/she left. Fairly soon it wont be as evident once you have got into step with the situation. TIME and more TIME, that thing that is present through the deployment.

You will work out the time zone difference very accurately too and it will become the most natural thing whenever you look at any clock or watch during their tour. Automatically, without having to work it out, their time will pop into your head.

CONTACT ISN'T TOO BRILLIANT

Lots of things have to be put into perspective. You may not hear from them often. You have oodles of time to put pen to paper or send messages in other forms whenever the feeling comes upon you. They don't have much spare time. It wont be equal.

You may not hear from them at all in the first 2 weeks. Even throughout the tour with so many troops wanting to use the phone or use a computer there can be extremely long queues waiting for their turn. For computers they have to book a time to use it. Those items are very much in demand. If you do hear from them in those first couple of weeks then you are very lucky indeed. In that time they have to settle in and take over from the regiment they are replacing. They have to get the routine that fits their regiments' requirements the best. They have to learn the camp layout and the area of the towns and nooks and crannies that they will be patrolling. Depending on where they are can be totally different as no camp is the same. It could be massive it could be small. Some may be well set up while others are pretty raw and in the making. Improvements will have to be done. If they are based in a FOB (forward operating base) the places are very small and very basic indeed with no ways to contact. That will be a very long and lonely waiting time. But wherever they are the shifts will be very long, sometimes 18-hour days, so that they barely have time to eat and catch a few hours sleep. They work very hard indeed from the moment the tour begins right through to the end with little relief at all. Gruelling. Fitting into their complicated schedule is not an easy step. They have to get used to working in full kit and carrying huge weights on their backs plus a very heavy weapon in these extreme temperatures of 50c must be torture. Now that is heat you will never have to experience.

Hooray our country has no such extremes. After all we moan when it rains. To us too wet and we wish there was sunshine. We moan if its hot.... phew that's overpowering or drying up our gardens so that our flowers don't grow and shrivel. We wish then it would rain for us. Petty problems that either way it just isn't right for us.

I am sure few of us could live in such unimaginable temperatures our troops have, never mind work in it. Everything is new to them and they are stuck in an alien and unwelcoming place. They could be on a different planet. Very unlike the home life they are used to. They are probably very home sick. Not only missing family and friends but their clean cosy homes where they don't have to suffer sand in their bed or clothes. They swap their fancy bathrooms for extremely basic washing facilities and loos. Life is no picnic. It is definitely no ordinary camp and very unlike their camp here. Be thankful your surroundings haven't changed.

These thoughts of how cruel it is out there for them fades a lot because what will be nagging at you are the problems that you have to manage to overcome every hour of every day at home. It is constantly in the forefront of your mind. It takes you over body and soul. Daily the twists and turns have a grip on you and as hard as you try to push them aside there is no shaking them off. It is a real tackle in all directions of the problems that never seem to pass. The wondering if you are strong enough to push your way through these trying times that seems to have no end. There appears to be no sight of the light at the end of the vast tunnel.

Playing a rugby match describes your situation best. All of the injuries, bruises, the fighting of other people, the dodging of the bad parts you are amidst, but also the great elation that flows through it when you score well.

Your house, your home, the family and friends and all parts of your lifestyle alters. It completely changes in a way you never thought was possible. This abnormal way now becomes the normal way. This is your Battle at home. However, your emotional side will probably calm down a bit so that all the crying is better controlled. Sorry to say the whole tour is very hard but you will find ways of coping with the situation a little easier as the tour progresses.

You can socialise and go wherever you choose whenever you want to although socialising could very well wane. You can phone your family or friends, any time of the day or night, when you are at a low ebb. There will be low ebbs all the way through when you will fall apart and you are going to need a great deal of support throughout this scary and longest roller coaster ride you have ever been on. Your naivety couldn't picture all of this and so the way things are going was far from anything you expected. A roller coaster you can't jump off. The ups and the downs. Some days will be better than others but there are the nerves and an enormous empty hole inside you that cannot be filled or understood by not only you but others too.

You have shoulders to cry on. There are people to hug and get hugs in return. You can have unrestricted tantrums and storm about and cry as often as you want to. Your soldier can't do any of those things. Where is their shoulder to cry upon? They have nobody to hug which means all their emotions are bottled up inside so that at times they explode and you are the one who gets it in the neck. You are their verbal punch bag to unleash their problems upon. So make allowances for their moodiness if there are times when you cant diagnose some unfriendly, niggly or very picky situation. Tantrums, yelling and screaming is something our troops cannot do or their job would go down the drain for sure. The best you can do is write, phone or e them as often as possible despite the horrific frustration of getting little in return. You are sending tons with few replies back. It doesn't seem at all fair but it's something you will have to get used to. It is a big thing to accept, or more likely try to accept, to enable you to arrange the situation into some sort of familiar order that can make a definite marker post to take with you when the same feeling swallows you up at any time. Put it in your pocket of understanding so that you can lean upon its strength should there be another identical problem of that same unfair feeling.

You are their life's blood and the most important link to home and sanity for them. Every single contact means so much to you and to them to bring smiles to faces. Try to imagine big time all of the love you send with every word and every e. Every phone call. Every parcel. Knowing how things are going at home is very important to them. I am sure you will have little grumbles about them under your breath for non-contact many times. OK that's normal because we all tend do it. Therefore have no guilt trip on that. You may vent a lot of anger often when you get so little back and you are thinking they don't care. You are so wrong because inside they are stirred up because they have no contact from you. You fume so much and blame so much. This is war. Never anything is regular and situations can change in an instant. When eventually they do get the opportunity to get to you in some way then this is the time they need loving and caring from you. Their morale needs boosting constantly because it means things are bad out there and they are doing their job. Work hard not to blame him/her as it isn't their fault. They are relying on you to get them out of their low esteem and lack of confidence that they now have. Of course the time has torn at your emotions but don't be selfish. He/she is feeling torn just like that but also in a dangerous and horrible place. Heck, do they need you. You are the reliable cuddles he/she knows you can give to them to get him/her back to his/her bouncy and happier self.

LINES DOWN

Another bugbear that you will have to face is a thing called "Lines Down". With no contact you start to get your knickers in a twist and the running around being a newsaholic trying to get as much information as possible takes its toll. You attach yourself to the television anxiously waiting for some unpleasant news that may have happened. Flicking the channels to check and recheck to find out if there is a piece on the news saying that there has been an incident. If the camp where your soldier is close to a place where something has happened then your mind goes berserk wondering if it could have affected him/her. Was he/she involved? Could he/she be in hospital? Oh the dread of that! Your imagination is filling your mind with horrors wondering if he/she is hurt or injured in some particular way. Your head is buzzing with as many reasons for not hearing. You keep on looking at your phone to see if there is a missed message on it. Could it have rung while you were in the loo or having a bath? You could have nipped out to the shops and its rung. Oh heavens that would be dreadful if you hadn't heard it at some point. You may be searching in your e-mails just in the vague hope that all of a sudden a message is now there for you. You might phone relatives or friends to ask if they have heard anything bad that as yet they have been too upset to get round to telling you. At least you now know your phone is working so that can't be the reason for no call from him/her. Whatever is the reason? You are getting desperate now. Out come the tissues again. Staring at the phone still willing it to ring is about as good as "A watched pot never boils" There sometimes can be an easy explanation for this non contact which is all to do with rules. Yes, more rules. Sensible rules of course. Safety rules. Take deep breaths and chill out if you can. Another easy thing to say but so very hard to do. "Lines Down" is when all of the phones and computers are disabled or banned. The reason could be due to unrest with the civilians or with the enemy. If there are injuries or if the camp is having difficulties then "Lines Down" is used. Various times it is put into operation. They pull out all the stops for safety, safety and more safety as no messages or news can be sent out. This may continue for several days until everything can be put back to normal. Absolutely no information can be allowed in or out for you to get to know lines are down. Security is paramount so that nothing at all is leaked accidentally.

Now amidst all of your traumatic behaviour do take all those reasons into account as to it being a very big possibility that it could be any one of the "Lines Down" reasons. He/she will get to you as soon as possible. The moment they can contact you once the rule is over then they definitely will. He/she must hate it as much as you do. They must be so upset with no way to let you know they are fine. No News is Good News. Always cling to that. They will be praying that the "Lines Down" will be finished quickly. It's a toughie when it's hyping you up. It's the trying to comprehend that rips you apart and stresses you out. After it has happened a few times then you will get more used to it. One of many incidents that join the "Waiting Game" situation. Keep thinking positively and get that attitude well stuck into your memory. Create happy vibes.

SENDING A BLUEY/LETTER

A "Bluey" is like an airmail letter but specially for the troops only. They are free and no postage is required. They have been pre-paid so it costs you nothing at all.

All post office people are so very helpful indeed and so you rely on them to help you through any of your postal doubts. They will give you all the right advice. However like all things in life it doesn't always go quite to plan. You can get a few post office people who can be unhelpful dragons and stare at you blankly or start up an argument thinking that you will bow to their knowledge. Stick to your guns and be firm because they too can be ignorant on various points. This minor hiccup can spoil your day. You have enough worries without this to be thrown headlong at you so that you flounder and lose a lot of confidence. They know what you are asking for but should they really give you more than one bluey at a time? Yes they should as it is your right. If they get stroppy with you then ask them to check it on their computer. That shuts them up when they see that you are right and they are wrong.

Smile sweetly in the post office and they should give you a handful of Blueys for you to take home so you can write at any time be it day or night when the feeling strikes you. There will be extremely silly hours when the urge is upon you to put pen to paper. You will be sending loads through the tour so it is a relief that they are free lol!

Make sure you address it correctly. It is no good making an error on that. When putting on the address this should include with it the rank, name and his/her army number. The BFPO number is like a postcode for the country and various camps. That is essential. Do not put on the country it is going to.

BFPO = British Forces Post Office

They take approximately one week to get there. It can take longer as TIME is very variable indeed when you wish it could be exact. All mail can be slow if there are backlogs or especially if he/she is not in a main camp. If he/she is out on an operation then he/she has to return to camp before he/she can get them.

That is the outside dealt with now let us see what you can write on the inside.

Obviously it is going to be full of love and hugs in the chat. Sloppy talk. Pillow talk. You will ask him/her how he/she is. If you are writing to your other half you will want to know how well he/she is coping without sex and how you are feeling with the lack of that too. It is a two way street because they are as frustrated as you. Soon you will be used to its absence. What do they do each day and what is the place like so that you can imagine more clearly the layout of the camp. Of course there will be lots of chat on how much you miss them. All that goes without saying. But they are going to need more meat in that sandwich.

Fill it with fun things that will make him/her laugh because he/she needs his/her sides to ache with comical bits and pieces. Smiles and giggles are marvellous to send or to receive so it will become morale boosting winging it's way across hundreds of miles to and from you both. Another important part of your learning curve added to. In writing it you too will find it uplifting, boosting and help you to brighten up your day. So you see that contact by bluey is a double bonus.

Mundane and everyday chitchat of your day's diary should be told. Where you have been even if it's just the shops you went to or taking and fetching the kids from school. Say what the kids or other members of the family have been doing. What the kids have been up to is important. Did anyone phone you or did you have a friend visit or perhaps you went to have a cuppa with a friend. If you go out for the day or evening with friends then tell them that. You mustn't become a recluse. Sitting back in your armchair and doing nothing isn't going to help you at all. Fill up your day by doing as much as possible. Your soldier may be rather jealous at first that you can go out and he/she can't. Don't take notice of their moans because soon jealousy won't come in to the picture and he/she will be happy that you are happy. They will enjoy reading about the things you do. They might dread that your life has ground to a standstill if you don't go out and enjoy yourself at times.

I am sure it wont be long before something breaks e.g. washing machine, kettle, central heating on the blink or your computer is playing up. After all its sods law these things happen when you are alone to deal with it. News like that is a must. (They will laugh at your misfortune while you have been upset by it.) Such nuisances could really make you flap or be angry. That's more money out of your pocket to replace it or get somebody in to mend it. Geez, it is so typical for everything that was so perfect before, now is totally imperfect which puts a strain on your day. You never thought about a nuisance like that. It is all part and parcel of you learning how to do things by yourself. Aren't you so glad that you kept note of the phone numbers of various helpful people to come to your aid. That really was a plan to help you out. At the time it probably seemed one of those things on the list that you were sure would never be of any use to you. If you haven't the phone numbers you will be digging through Yellow Pages or asking a friend if they know a reliable and trustworthy company to do the job best at the same time possibly the cheapest too. Try to steer clear of "cowboys" who could make the job worse than it was. Expect the unexpected when making out the list before he/she left. Phoning up the repairman doesn't always work out right because they may not be able to come and repair or correct the problem the next day. It could be many days so things will not be fixed as fast as you want. That is another problem to deal with. The date and time hopefully will be when you want it so that you do not have to stop in waiting at some inconvenient hour or cancel something that was already planned. Lets face it we do know how painful it can be to get them out! How the heck are you going to manage with a broken this, that or other in the meantime? Here is a reason for you to go cherry red with anger and be quite in the mood to pull your hair out. Whoops here come those tears again. The awful trail to the shops to buy or order a new item. Even just the thought of having to do that gets up your nose. The checking of your bank account to see if you can afford a big item. Is there sufficient to pay for it? Not at all easy when it all seems so complicated. However, wont you be able to make them proud of you when you write to say that yes you got it all sorted out. You will make yourself proud that you actually got through that rough patch.

You may have an accident e.g. where you tripped and fell over and ripped your tights or cut and bruised yourself. Perhaps you have put something red in with the wash and it all came out pink. Oh happy days when these things happen! To your soldier this is all news to keep them closer to the usual life back home.

Give them the latest gossip. Football team scores or other things they are interested in. Get a list of where matches are to be played or perhaps things about racehorses with their favourite jockey. It is part of home situations that need to fill him/her up. It creates the idea that there is less distance to the natural world he/she longs for.

Should there be any miserable news to send then keep what you write of that to a minimum and don't dwell on it or keep going on about it in bluey after bluey. Play it down but never try to hide it. Your soldier is not a baby who you have to wrap in cotton wool. Imagine if the boot was on the other foot. Would you want information hidden from you? It won't ring true if you say that life for you doesn't have a single blip in it.

These blueys are meant to boost them up and for stashing them under his/her pillow or in a uniform pocket. He/she most probably will read them over and over and will know them off by heart. He/she probably will fall asleep while reading them and they act as an enormous hug. These letters mean so much. You have knitted together a bluey that will wrap around him/her like a comfort blanket. Just the getting of one and imagining what's in it puts soldiers on a terrific high. It is a ginormous something from home. Their morale is even more boosted when they read it. They will probably talk to their mates about the news they have. Sharing the latest information from home is big and fun and lots of things to discuss with their friends and giving each other the updates of all the natter from home.

Here is a poem written by Kenneth James Garrick who sent this to his girlfriend soldier when she was out in Afghanistan.

ON HOLD

Put my life on hold for to battle you've gone

For me there's no joy, there's no happy song

My heart has been ripped from my body now cold

For the fear is too great that you'll never grow old

What do I do in the silence of night?

God give me strength and some of your mite

Fake smiles have I now and no I'm not proud

For I am lost to the fear that covers like a shroud

Where do I go, to whom do I turn

When of your fate I wish to learn

Whitehall does not care of the ones left behind

Nor of it's soldiers who it treats so unkind

We are all fighting battles, ours in our mind

And we have no weapons or brothers in kind

The mail is all that says for now you are well

But of your well-being there is no way to tell

You are amazing people, the best that there is

But now that you're gone I am all in a tiz

Please come back safe to where you belong

And until that day I will try to be strong.

That poem seems to be one from the heart which was written at the time when Kenneth must have deeply thought about his particular feelings at that time and all of the problems, hopes and love that looked at him every day in one way or another. The contents were releasing the points that were troublesome and questioning and in the forefront of his mind. He relieved all of his pent up feelings so that he un-bottled them in a way that he found was perfect for him. This was a flow of poetry that his girl friend loved getting with most of the letters that he wrote. Poems that helped them both to understand.

Most people wont do any poetry at all but it is just a gem of an idea that perhaps you could try to do even if it ends up in the bin and never sent. On this roller coaster there is never any harm in trying to experiment with different types of things that may work or go down like a lead balloon.

Getting all the things put into writing relieves you considerably by filling it with stuff of every minute and every hour in each day that has gone on. Not just the content but also the fact that you have put pen to paper even if your writing isn't exactly very neat or if it is a nasty scrawl. We can't all have decent handwriting! The time you took to write it just for them is very important.

You may think that these very petty pieces of information are not worth saying but they are. It's the little things that mean a lot and gives them huge smiles to see one has arrived. That is why it is good to keep those blueys sent often.

How many times will you dash down stairs straight to the letterbox to see if a bluey has come to you. If one hasn't then you will probably check and check again with the idea Mr Postie perhaps did his round late or somehow left your mail in the bottom of his sack. Your imagination goes daft trying to conjure up the different ways something wasn't delivered. But there will be times when hey presto something has arrived. Just don't fall down the stairs in your excitement to get to it! Opening that bluey can't be done quickly enough. Then of course once you have stopped shouting it from the rooftops to say "Yippee I have a Bluey". And reading it really does put you onto another "high". You treasure every word written. Oh my, you may even phone a friend or relative to give them your wonderful news. After all it's not just any old piece of mail. It's a special piece of mail worth gold dust. Everyone must know about it. If you feel this way then imagine how the mail you send is going to be loved equally.

OK it seems pointless and upsetting as the blueys in response to all those that you send out definitely do not match the few that you get. Tears will flow due to this upset and tension. This doesn't balance by any means. This must be in your thoughts but in the meantime always be trying so very hard to accept you will get a minimum. It's that old chestnut called TIME. You have so much spare time to allow you to write and they don't get many chances to answer. You have lots to write about whereas each day is the same for him/her. Give them a nudge now and again to write to you more if they can squeeze in an incy bit extra if at all possible. But bless them they may not be able to do it no matter how much you wish they could. It might not even register with them that you need blueys from them too. Typical man doesn't consider such things. So the odd elbow to remind them could help if thoughtlessness is their only reason not to.

I am very sure that any blueys you get will be kept handy or even under your pillow. This is your comfort blanket. You may show them to your friends or family to read when they drop in or read them to them over the phone. You will also know all of those blueys off by heart. Read and re read so many times. They are priceless. To cuddle up in a chair with a big hot drink to read them over and over even if you are watching TV or video you will still have them next to you for peeping and peeping and putting you on a high at any time. Printing out your e-mails gives you more to snuggle up to.

How far a journey has it come to drop through your letterbox? Just contemplating that is awesome. It is better still if other relatives and friends could write too. The more the merrier. So plant the idea in their minds to get into the habit of writing to your sweetie when they can.

There is a forfeit that seems to be a soldier's very own rule of thumb. The soldier who gets the most mail each week has to buy a crate of pop to share out between the others with less mail. I have no doubt they wish it was a crate of beer but alcohol is illegal so pop is the only thing ha ha! A forfeit nonetheless.

HOLD UPS WITH ALL MAIL

You will realise that the getting mail, be it blueys or parcels, can be far from easy. That means in both directions. It's hard enough with our ordinary mail inland so to or from a war zone then has very difficult hurdles that complicate it. This is when patience is a virtue.

You post it at your post office or post-box and then it has to be taken to the military airport from where it is flown out. That's the easy bit. If you can call that easy when its just started on its way.

There may be a backlog. After all, the tonnes that gets sent out daily puts a pressure on the people getting it on board. The loading and the unloading of it. A truly difficult task but be assured they do their very best. All mail is sent via military planes and from a military airport.

Weather can hold up the planes so they can't take off in the way that any plane has to be concerned with weather en route.

Obviously they can only fly out to a war zone if it is safe to land or from there it has to be safe to take off in order to get here.

When the mail arrives over there it then has to be unloaded and sorted once again for the various camps that it has to go to. Then the Posties have to deliver it to them risking life and limb along their various routes to each camp which can be in different areas. There is the easier to get at as well as the extremely difficult which takes longer with fewer chances to be able to deliver.

Once at the camp it has to be sorted again. Not until then can the troops get it.

There are places where no mail can be taken at all. Also no phone calls if they are out on an operation that could last days or a couple of weeks. The troops have to wait until they get back to their base camp in order to receive it or send any out. It is very tough on them but also tough on you because being without contact can pull you down quite a lot. You can happily imagine though the heap of mail and parcels that greet them if they have been out on an operation.

Please consider all of these difficulties there are regarding its journey. Trying to be patient is very hard. Another addition to be added to your learning curve. That is why there can never be exact travelling times but only approximate ones.

Be happy that they can actually get mail. If you look at WW2 it was rare that any mail could be sent or received. If very lucky then it was only a few times a year. No computers had been developed then and no phones wherever the troops were for them to use. Only very sleepy snail mail letters, which were checked and censored thoroughly, which meant various things in them were crossed out which were considered unsuitable.

NO NEWS IS GOOD NEWS if there are delays. Keep saying this to yourself to calm yourself because it is true. Simple reasons for haphazard arrivals for what to you must only be huge problems will have a very ordinary reason that you never even thought about. No news from officials is good news.

THE LETTER YOU WISHED YOU HADN'T SENT

You must be honest on this point because you will send at least one letter that you so regret writing and should never have been put near the post-box let alone put in the post-box! After chewing it over in your mind you want to kick yourself for it. It is too late when you realise it is a knee jerk reaction where you have made something minor into something major. There is no Dr Who machine for you to step into so that you can go backwards to the time you hadn't sent it. You do so wish there could be one because the moment that letter slips from your hand and is posted you suddenly wish so very hard you hadn't. Off it goes full of venom to reach your soldier. There are thousands of reasons this was written in the first place. Was it to blame for the situation of him/her making you suffer all of this because of the career? Could it be because of love annoyances? Could it be that you feel your relationship is falling apart? Accusations may abound of unfaithfulness. Was it pure anger with a great mix of things that has blown into one unmanageable heap? Has your soldier barely written to you? That is a real wind up when with all your letters you have sent but little comes to you. Are any letters to you very short and not as lovingly written as you wish they could be? Whatever the tale is, it has now been sent. To put it in a nutshell your emotions have boiled over. You got flaming mad and now you resemble Satan's looks. Horns coming out of your head, red faced and snarling teeth are not unnoticeable. A spur of the moment knee-jerk reaction with little thought behind it caused you to write the most horrible words that will rip raw nerves the moment it is opened. Now you grit your teeth and inwardly hurt like mad for being such a "plonker". So you now see that the nasty bluey you have sent has thrown itself back at you. Why oh why could you have not waited for a few hours more or till the following day to post when all of your anger may very well have cooled off? You will wonder why you even got bloody mad in the first place. That's the time when nine times out of ten you will wish you had binned it and you will be so upset you were daft enough to post. Then and only then if you still want to vent your feelings then do so. If you still feel you might burst then decide if it's right to be sent. Only you can judge.

If they were home you could row hammer & tongs, banter back and forth, make a compromise or one of you clearly wins hands down. Something of that ilk at least. Then it is all over and done with quickly. However, sending anger in message form is not the most brilliant of things to do. Worry and guilt churns over and over inside knowing full well that a reaction to it will take a week to know its final result. You have punished yourself. You have opened a huge can of worms that has lashed back at you in everyway possible and he/she hasn't even got it yet. You think over what the result will be and the dreadful reply you could get back. That is if you get a reply at all as you may have burnt your boats in one full sweep for a while at least. How did your soldier take it? Emotions have been stirred. Perhaps this mess you have made will wash over him/her. Can it be resolved? Might a speedy letter explaining your actions that you were feeling very low at the time help? What if you try to say you had a bad hair day. Would an "I am sorry" letter fix it? It could need a lot of sweet mail back and forth to securely get things back on track. Take into account that angry letters work both ways as he/she may have a bad hair day and at some point be the one to send the same type to you.

Sending an angry e or ebluey must be treated in a similar way. Do not hit "SEND". Pull your finger away from that magnetic button. Save it. Think it over carefully. Perhaps make a cuppa and sit down. Watching TV or going for a walk might be good ideas. Anything to relax you in the best way for you. Remember to breathe. Huge breaths in through the nose and very very slowly out of the mouth while having pursed lips. That can have a calming effect.
Have the resilience to wait until the following day. It is always best to

decide once you have cooled off. Most times you will shock yourself as to why you wrote such a rotten e which gives you the opportunity to delete it. Heartache will be avoided and no can of worms opened. If there is ever anger the best way to deal with it is by the use of a telephone when it can be chewed over sensibly and adultly by you both with no waiting time. This way works the best. Try to compromise if the problem can't be cleared up. Agree to differ. Discussion is nearly always best. Screaming down the phone resolves nothing and gets you even more upset.

READING MAIL WHEN YOU FEEL LOW

As you know there are days when you are feeling so low that nothing can cheer you up. Even mail you get can give a bad effect on you. You are meant to be so very happy to get it until you read it and then all hell breaks loose. It isn't because it's a nasty one but you turn it into one. You read between the lines and the most loving things irk you. I can only warn you that it can be commonplace but hopefully only on rare occasions. Fingers crossed it wont even happen. Out comes that box of tissues that you will now need. You pull each sentence apart one by one and wonder if the sentence means what the words convey. You begin to think that it was written for your benefit but could be totally untrue. The next sentence and then the next until in your mind you think it must be a total sham. Being low makes all your thoughts exaggerated and gruesome. You can be so gripped with the upset you have built and now cannot control. You will eventually realise you had your stupid head on but not before you have got stressed. Not until you have bawled your eyes out and gone through so many tissues. You will have paced up and down with emotions of anger and upset surging forth and digging its claws in. You may scream and act in some awful ways. You will swear a lot and make the air blue. Not until lots of wild emotions that have been thrown into your imagination and eventually thrown out again will you be at peace. You now realise you were such an idiot. Heck, weren't you just!

Accept any loving and sweet mail as true. Don't twist it to mean it's something different. Never be stupid and turn it upside down. It causes moods that you would be better without.

SENDING A PARCEL

This seems a complicated thing to do but you will find it not at all frightening after you have sent your first so don't fret. It will become a natural and easy thing to do. Nothing at all as complex as you may have at first thought. The idea of sending it exactly right can worry you but take heart on its simplicity. No negative brain straining stresses. Another "Wherever do I start" part of the learning curve is all it is.

All parcels must not weigh more than 2kg. Perhaps you should invest in a very accurate pair of scales. Parcels go free, yippee, so be sure to weigh it correctly. It is a big shame if when you take it to the Post Office and it is even slightly overweight they will make you undo your beautifully, safely, securely wrapped parcel and you have to open it and remove an item. Ruined before your very eyes. It is so upsetting in many ways. It isn't too brilliant if there are other customers looking at you. It can be heartbreaking. It will make you angry too. All of the things that you have taken time over to pack so that nothing moves about and out has to come an item from the parcel to make it lighter. Out come your tissues to mop those tears and wipe your nose. Steam coming out of your ears isn't at all attractive either and words may splurt out of your mouth to ensure your feelings are heard as well as seen.

Address the parcel clearly and correctly. Write in big letters the BFPO with its number. It is a type of postal code for the country, area and camp. Do not write the countries name on it. Write your address on the back of the parcel in smaller writing. This is in case it goes astray or you have addressed it incorrectly. It can then be posted back to you. If it contains illegal items it will also be returned to you or destroyed.

You will be given a label to write on its contents. You don't have to be precise. So just put e.g. Toiletries, sweets, books, or food. The Post Office will advise you on this if you are unsure. Then you stick the label on your parcel. Ask for a few labels to take home as filling them in at home saves a lot of hassle for the rest of the queue behind you. If your PO doesn't have these labels (many don't have them) then write the contents on the parcel itself for this will suffice.

Forces' aircraft take all BFPO mail and parcels. So the above instructions are not too complicated as you probably imagined it was going to be. Pretty straight forward. The correct weight. Their address, your address and list of contents. Simplicity itself. Some Post Offices sell flat pack boxes that you can buy. However a handy thing to use instead for a perfect and free box is to go to a shoe shop and ask for any spare shoeboxes they have. They are only too happy to help you. They are the ideal size. Remember to cushion the items so that they don't roll around in the box and it helps to prevent breakages. Bubble wrap or newspaper is excellent to fill in any gaps. The extra boost for you is that you are happy with its contents so that it is off to your loved one. Woohooo. Then do a merry dance when you hear that it has arrived. Only you can guess the joy on his/her face and the many things yelped with great delight even before it is opened.

FOR SECURITY PURPOSES ALL PARCELS WILL BE X-RAYED FOR CONTENT.

WHAT PARCELS DO FOR YOUR SOLDIER

All parcels lift every soldier's spirits absolutely to unbelievable heights. It is definitely positive that anything sent will be treasured or eaten very fast. Greedy guts. They invariably share things with a mate or two. It causes smiles, love and sentimental rushes with memories of family and home. Love really does pour out from it. It isn't just the contents but knowing that you wrapped the parcel. Every item included was chosen by you and specially thought about. The fact that you went around the shops looking for the things they like and the more fun things that will make them laugh. The items you know are a must for them regarding practical goods required. Edibles will make them lick their lips. Yummy! Whatever it may be or its size of contents doesn't matter,(remember the 2kg weight) as equal love will come from it. Tears of happiness may roll down their cheeks. Special tears for the things chosen by the kids. It will be warming to get paintings they have done. It pulls at the heartstrings in such a lovely way. Photos of you, the family and friends and of home and garden. Anything you know they will get that extra kick from. They like to lie back on their beds and look at them time and time again to make them oh so happy. Woohoo! Photos are a great comfort. You can now see the importance of parcels.

Parcels take from 2 to 3 weeks to arrive but its that TIME game again which you cannot rely on.

They will be shouting it from the barrack roof in the same way that you will be shouting it from your rooftop when he/she sends something to you. It could be chocolates or flowers delivered. Everything is a two way street. They will want to make you feel special if they get such an opportunity to send something. "TIME" raising its head again. Do not worry if it takes longer or if they arrive out of sequence.

WHAT TO PUT IN MY PARCEL

You can send whatever you choose but it's always handy to have a lot of ideas to prompt you. In your first one you may include things that are rolling round your brain making you wonder if they forgot to take certain items. If they already have got it then they can save it. Clothing isn't necessary although undies, t-shirt or socks are fine and now and again useful due to excessive usage. Ask them to tell you when they need them. I think you get my drift. Keep in mind that they have very little room to put things, as mainly it is just a bed space. Food in cans is not recommended as it is heavy and takes up a lot of space. You will spot things when you are out shopping that might be a "something" that they might like to get. I am very sure you will notice such things. Put in silly fun items. Making up the parcels will put you on cloud 9. You will enjoy putting them together. Read the following suggestions as ideas for you to use.

USEFUL, FUN AND LOVING ITEMS TO SEND

A WHITE HANKY.. With lipstick kisses all over it so they can have your kisses close to their heart. You can also spray a little bit of your perfume on it. This adds to its lovability.

CRISPS, NIBBLES AND SNACK ITEMS.. Their favourite ones that they munch on at home. Be it Quavers, Crisps, Twiglets, Chipsticks etc

BISCUITS.. You may even consider making your own although I am sure there are so many bought types that home made is rare. Especially by me as I am a rotten cook!!! I can't see my son eating my attempts though as they may only be suitable to feed to the camels.

CAKES.. Definitely only the ones that don't melt or go sticky. In all things you send heat is a nuisance factor. Pack so that it can't move about or get smashed up.

POT NOODLES.. Quite a favourite.

CEREALS.. Those individual mini boxes to have as a snack at anytime. Check first if they have enough milk available. Find out the situation. They could take them to add or have at breakfast time.

RAISINS AND SULTANAS.. They can eat these on their own but also they can put some with the cereal. So many varieties of dried fruits can be got from health food stores.

SWEETS.. Haribos are very addictive to the soldiers because they all adore them and will ask you always to send more and more of them.

Various other types but be sure…has it sunk in… they must not be the type that melt. Chocolate makes a horrible mess and melts en route. Truly a sorry mucky mush. It melts in the hand before it reaches the mouth. You don't want the gunky stuff to be a part of the contents they get. Temperatures can be a very real problem.

MINTS.. They refresh the mouth and Polo's are a popular favourite as they are easy to carry in a uniform pocket when they are out on patrol.

CHEWING GUM.. Another refreshing item and cleans the mouth. It is another easy thing for his/her pocket.

SACHETS OF POWDER/CRYSTAL DRINK FLAVOURINGS.. The troops have to drink 10-15 litres of bottled water daily to prevent dehydration in the severe heat which is typical in Iraq and Afghanistan. So much water is bland so these flavouring sachets are adored to add to some of it. They can be bought in chemists. Lucozade flavour can be bought in Boots and many other flavours can be bought from other chemists. Some supermarkets sell them too. These additions make it healthier as well as flavoursome. They assist in the prevention of dehydration and really do help a great deal because of the contents essential additives included in them. To send these is very important.

Search about to find who sells them near you.

They can be bought online:

www.ekmpowershop3.com

Postage for them is cheap

It is never good to send those isotonic bottles of drink as they congeal into a sticky glue. The content of those is mainly sugar and do not really help at all. A typical sales hype with silly unfounded promises. Plus any bottles of drink are very stupid because of its weight and the space it takes up when they get it.

TEA.. Send their favourite type or experiment by sending different types of tea and see which ones are preferred. It could be an interesting result with really unusual ones such as herbal.

COFFEE.. Send out different types. You never know this could be fun.

COCOA/DRINKING CHOCOLATE/HORLICKS.. Any other type of drinks of a similar nature that you can think of. Hot drinks can be as cooling as cold ones. An unusual piece of interesting information.

ICE POPS.. Most have mini fridges and I am sure that all will enjoy them when they are frozen and icy cold and into their mouths. Frozen heaven. Yummy.

SUN CREAM/OIL.. Preferably over factor 15. They want a tan but not to be sore. Fairly soon their body gets accustomed to the sun and they won't need it.

AFTER SUN.. To protect them or relieve them if they are sore. Sun can be a hazard. Sometimes it can be very painful.

CHAP STICK.. Another way to protect them. We are most surely in the protection racket.

BABY WIPES.. I suggest the non-perfumed type. I can't see the blokes wanting to smell like a baby but you never know they just might. They really are cooling and refreshing to use as face and body wipes. They are ideal to get sand from every bodily crevice where it can collect! Every soldiers dream. Keep these as top priority and send them as often as they need them. He/she can put them beside the bed to wipe their faces as necessary.

WET NAPS INDIVIDUALLY WRAPPED.. Very handy to carry in their pocket.

HAND HELD FANS.. Some have a water mister.

TOILETRIES.. Shower gel

> Soap
>
> Shampoo
>
> After shave
>
> Cologne
>
> Shaving soap
>
> Deodorants …no aerosols
>
> Make-up and perfume for the ladies

These items are essential to make their very sweaty selves to smell sweeter and refresh them. Foot gel might help their tired tootsies!! Foot powder is welcomed with glee. Their feet can get very sore with bacterial problems so this powder is a very helpful item. Don't send too much too often or he/she can end up with mountains of toiletries that can't be got through and waste their small space.

It is better if you put the liquid items in a plastic bag so that if there are any unfortunate leakages it won't mess up the other contents in the parcel.

MOISTURISER or BABY OIL.. Their skin dries out very swiftly so replenishing the moisture is a boon

MAGAZINES.. They are very handy to pass round and share when they are finished with them. This way they are never short of magazines to read. They share things a lot. A case of "read it and pass it on"

LOCAL NEWSPAPER.. This keeps him/her in touch with their town. If you don't want to send the whole paper then cut out the rubbish pages of no interest. There is no need to send National papers as they have those out there.

SPORTS RESULTS.. Or interests in any footy or other sports. You could send them badges or small flags of the team they support.

BOOKS.. The type that you know he/she loves. These occupy their free time and relaxes their minds. Another item they can pass on to their mates after they have read it. Also ones on any particular interests they may have. Go to Charity shops and second hand book shops and buy them from there. They are very cheap and browsing through them for the type he/she prefers can be quite interesting. New or expensive books are not recommended unless it is a specific one that is wanted. You may come across books that you too would enjoy reading.

PUZZLE BOOKS.. Crosswords, word searches etc. As you know you can get the giant crossword books with hundreds inside which will take him/her a long time to complete.

JOKE BOOKS.. They can really make their sides ache and laughter is very catching. Equally there could be a lot of groans from their mates when they are rather unfunny or stale. Even the moans bring about a chuckle or two.

JOKES.. Go to your local joke shop and get some silly stuff, e.g. grow your own boobs plant, grow your own girlfriend. Anything that you think will give your love a real laugh. They always need something stupid. I am sure you will find allsorts of things to fit your soldiers' sense of humour. An endless variety. Fun is good for the system.

FRISBEES..It lets them have a great deal of enjoyable exercise.

PACK OF CARDS.. A very popular pastime. An excellent time filler for them playing solitaire or playing cards with their friends.

BOARD GAMES.. It is good if you get those mini hand held pocket ones that they can take anywhere with them. Remember that shortage of space.

i-POD.. Really does give them a relaxing element of their choice in music. They can lay back and look a goon. Doesn't everyone wearing headphones?

PERSONAL DVD PLAYER.. For those who have a camcorder then you can copy home movies of you and the kids. If they don't have a DVD personal player they can put them on to computers that are available on the camp. They are handy to show kids parties, baby's first steps; first day at school or anything that you think will be enjoyed. Keeps them in touch with home. (Never send expensive items in case the parcel goes astray or they break or worst still get stolen so only cheapo stuff that you won't cry over if something happens to it)

MINI CD PLAYER.. Send them their favourite CD's.. Again do not send too many. That space Grrrrrrr!

HAND HELD TAPE RECORDER.. Send tape messages of you and other members of the family and friends. You can have fun doing it and in return he/she can send you tapes of him/herself.

PHOTOS.. Tons of pictures of you and especially family orientated ones that are those of the home and garden and friends. Just whatever you think will be best suited.

MUGS.. Sensible, funny or cheeky. Buy a mug and personalise it by painting, writing or printing on it in the way that suits you. Don't worry if you are no fantastic artistic sort of person. It's done by you. That is always the important thing. Hooray. You will enjoy doing it and bring huge smiles when it's received. A lot of photographic shops have a machine to print onto objects. If you want to go to extremes then you can also get "make your own mug" kits from craft shops that will be a new experience for you. Children get great fun in being involved helping with this. Pack the mugs carefully to prevent breakage.

PLASTER IMPRINTS.. Of babies hands and feet for a parent to watch how they are growing. Babies grow so fast that you don't notice but its extra good to have them being a part of it too. Be sure to date them.

PAINTED HANDS AND FOOTPRINTS.. Use water paints to put on the children and press onto paper or card. It can be messy if baby curls up toes or fingers, as then there is a big possibility that you could end up with a lot of paint on you too! Send them painted a different colour each time. Don't send them every time or it wont let them guage the difference. Don't forget to write on the back the date on which each was done.

BABY SCANS.. If you are pregnant then send scan pictures. They can see baby develop the same as you. Photos of your bump as you grow too will be lovely. Put together the information given to you by the doctor and nurse as it all progresses.

PAINTINGS.. Ones done by the children or even you. Also the paintings that children do at school and bring home are a delight.

PREZZIES.. Items that the children have chosen themselves even if they are not exactly the sort of thing you might ever consider getting. It is the love that goes with it that counts. It does help to make the children involved with the content and it can be a very big bonus.

TEDDY BEAR or CUDDLY TOY.. It sounds silly but soldiers think they are cute especially if it has little messages on its tummy. They have a hard job to do but the soldiers are big softies at heart, full of gentleness and it's a special comfort link and something to snuggle up with. There are teddies that have a recording device inside so that every time he/she wants to hear your voice then it just needs a cuddle. A little spray on it of your favourite perfume/cologne can make it extra special. A finishing touch.

PARAPHERNALIA.. Cards that are suitable for any holiday, Birthday, Valentines Day, Easter, Christmas and Anniversaries. If you send Christmas Crackers then remove the explosive tabs. It sounds so drastic and idiotic but they are illegal. All the ammo the troops have and the Customs out there consider cracker tabs an explosive device! Nutty but true. It made my mind boggle when I first discovered that. Send tinsel to decorate their bed, Christmas stocking, Santa hat. A 6" fibre optic tree. Perhaps cards for no particular reason but for a show of love. For Birthdays send a cake and paper hats so they can have a little Birthday

Party with their friends. Those silly whistles are quite fun to mess about with. Keep his/her main presents until he/she gets home.

T-SHIRT.. You could have a photo of you printed on it or personalise it in other ways that might spring to mind. Write messages on it with fabric pens and get friends or other family to add to it. Sparkly pens can be bought for an added delight.

PILLOW CASE.. Get 2 and put a photo of you on the one you send and a photo of him/her on the one you keep. Some photographic shops have machines to print these on. A way to go off to bed with you having him/her in bed with you. A touch of perfume on it is sexy for the chap and if you put cologne/deodorant on to stir the ladies. It makes it a little bit more of a personal comfort. Very romantic indeed. You could ask him/her to take a photo of it on their bed.

UNDIES.. Boxer shorts, Y-fronts, pants, bras and socks. Do not inundate them but a good rule of thumb is to ask if they need new ones.

ST.CHRISTOPHER .. It is the patron saint for travellers. It seems a very appropriate item. Perhaps getting a matching pair so that you both have the same.

CRUCIFIX.. Religion may be very important to both of you so that can be very fitting.

POEMS.. You could try writing your own for him/her as a little sweetener. It may encourage them to write some to you. You might not be the greatest poet but its fun. Have a go. You may be very surprised at what you can do.

CARDS/POSTCARDS.. Make your own by designing them or using photos of family, friends and things home orientated. You could even buy some really humorous ones. Perhaps have a go at drawing caricatures or doing little pictures.

COMPOSE... A letter using words cut out of magazines and paste them on paper. A quirky hotchpotch of a letter indeed. It will look like some blackmail letter you might see in a whodunit film when they don't want their handwriting recognised. It's a different rather than the usual way.

FUN LETTER.. Write it as if it has been written by an object or pets point of view. Their car, golf clubs, the fridge or other favourite possession. Or use the theme that it has been written by a person in a certain profession. E.g. Nurse..Medical notes, Doctor.. Prescription, Teacher.. School report. Secretary.. Memo. Chef.. Menu. Others a CV or any that might spring to mind.

PUZZLE LETTER/PHOTO..Cut up a letter or photograph to make a puzzle for your soldier to solve the problem and put them together to read or see it.

SILK STOCKING.. Send a gorgeous silk stocking with a note saying he has to take care of it and find the other one when he gets back!

WISHBONE + RIBBON..Clean and dry the wishbone from your roast chicken and tie around a pretty ribbon saying "Wish you were here" It is little touches like this that mean so very much.

WW1 and WW2 ITEMS … look up on the Internet patriotic WW1 & WW2 pictures, postcards, cartoons, poems etc. Copy & send those that catch your eye. There are some lovely romantic & patriotic ones to be found.

WHAT YOU CAN'T SEND

NO AEROSOLS/pressurised canisters or carbonated/fizzy drinks. The pressure in the cargo hold is unstable and it can cause them to explode. It is a hazard and you wouldn't want to spoil yours or other peoples mail and packages.

NO SHARP OR BLADED ITEMS of any description.

NO ALCOHOL or PORN being caught will result in an extremely heavy fine or fine plus watching the item destroyed. It is certainly not worth taking the risk. Customs are very strict and impose these legal restrictions. Please realise that the Customs Police have the right to inspect parcels at random whenever they want to.

MEAT is a definite NO! It is not fit to send and no airports around the world will accept it. It is also a huge culture shock if they are found in some countries with certain religions.

NO FLAMMABLE FLUIDS such as lighter fuel.

CHRISTMAS PARCELS

These need to be sent about 5 weeks before Christmas to be sure they get there in time. This is the busiest time because so many parcels get sent out therefore those ones could arrive there much more slowly. That word regarding "TIME" once more!

A CHRISTMAS STORY

Christmas was such a laugh when people sent tinsel to hang round the beds. All the things to brighten up the barracks so that it really felt more than just other days. Every day is so much like each other that with all the cards and decorations it definitely in no uncertain terms showed that Christmas truly had come. It was amazing how many people sent Santa hats. It was hilarious. Imagine what they looked like wearing them when they did. Mmmmn, hard to envisage I expect. It could certainly look threatening to the enemy and would have them fleeing away! Christmas stockings to hang on the end of their beds with mini sized and fun gifts in. There are things called Santa Keys to hang up. These are essential. How else would Santa get in with them having no chimney? I was told that the items wrapped in Christmas paper or said "DO NOT OPEN UNTIL CHRISTMAS" were kept unopened without trying to nose in. Ok maybe little sneaky peeks or feels to guess what might be inside. They wanted to be opening them all together with their friends and workmates so that would mean a lot more with a bigger buzz. Saying WOW and other descriptive words as a team. Showing each other what they had got. They shared out the edibles so they really stuffed themselves silly. So cool to actually wait and open them together. Whether that was a white lie I can't guarantee. I had to laugh imagining our soldiers pulling the crackers minus the tab so that they would have to say "BANG". I suppose the equivalent to seeing a child go Brrm brrm when driving an imaginary car. The whole camp is Christmassy for sure. Those types of added contents are so important. They will be jumping around like schoolboys and girls and you will too when you open yours. Whatever you get you will be hyped up with such excitement. Happy and smiling for sure. Any parcel is a special occasion that all have to know about. You will be screaming and dancing around and phoning family and friends to let them know it all in great detail is so very irresistible. Not forgetting a Christmas phone call from your loved one, which tops things off nicely.

THEY DO HAVE THEIR OWN SHOP

Do not be too distressed because there is always a shop on the camp for them to buy food and other basic things. Try and find out if they can buy batteries etc because that will save you sending them. There is a wide selection of goods but specific brands e.g. as in toiletries then they may prefer a brand name that isn't stocked. Also they prefer to get a lot of things from home. A parcel from you and the enjoyment they get from delving into it to see what you have sent is so very much better. It's totally different for them rather than going to the camp shop with the basket, which is more of a chore than a fun event. But yes, they all do need to do there own shopping. Remember that the parcels you send shouldn't be essentials but extras.

PARCELS43 SUPPORTING OUR TROOPS

This is how free postage for parcels came about with Teresa Theobald who took the bull by the horns and made it happen. This is her story. The outcome that we all have to be so grateful for. If you want to bring about army welfare subjects that you feel should be worthy of a necessary improvement in some way then one port of call is to go to Teresa's website and ask for her advice and assistance. Perhaps you can bring it about by a petition with a chance to create a result.

This is the information from Teresa about her parcels petition.

"During the summer of 2007 families were feeling unsettled about the cost of sending parcels to their loved ones in Afghanistan and Iraq. Some parcels were containing just goodies however others were containing food items for those in forward bases who were enduring rations for months on end.

Families decided to turn to campaigning to see if they could make a difference ...others had also campaigned for this in the past and changes had failed to take place. A petition was launched on the Downing Street website and Parcels43 was launched as a campaign. Families were asked to write 'supporting Our Troops Parcels43' on all outgoing mail to their loved ones. This in turn was noticed at the Royal mail sorting office in central London.

A month later a website was launched and the group name changed to Parcels43 Supporting Our Troops, this name seemed to flow better with what we as a group were trying to achieve. Help was initiated throughout the country and co-ordinators took on media coverage of our petitioning with local papers.

The East Anglian Daily Times came to my house to get the story and the day it went to press the national papers also picked up on the fact that food parcels were being sent to some troops. I myself was also invited onto GMTV and asked about the parcels that families were sending.... I myself had wanted to send what ever was needed by my son and sent all manner of things from wet wipes to sandals to pot noodles to flapjacks, it wasn't just about food items it was about the cost of postage involved to some families who were less able to pay.

A few days after appearing on GMTV a senior Army officer appealed to Royal Mail to carry parcels to the military sorting office free of charge, within days this was implemented though at this point just up until the normal Christmas free post. Campaigning carried on as normal at this point as we had no idea of what would happen after that point. I had word it was to be made permanent in advance of the announcement and everyone was overjoyed with the outcome.

The £6.50 families had been paying to post each parcel could now go towards paying for the contents of each box winging its way to loved ones serving in sandy places. Personnel can now relax in the knowledge that their families are not having to go without to ensure they get a little something from home.

The Parcels43 website upgraded in Dec 2007 to a professional website, our designer has no military connections but just wanted to help us. We also had the new addition of a forum which runs 24/7, it is moderated but also instantly uploading allowing help when help is needed. We are public domain so anyone is able to view so you must always be careful not to post anything that could cause a risk to yours or the security of others.

As a group we host different campaigns set up by others as well as those we also take on ourselves, above all though Parcels43 Supporting Our Troops is about one thing and that's 'Support'.

We are made up of loved ones of personnel and aim to support all who contact us in any way we can.

We would like to see Free Post for all on active deployment as we feel that hardships are endured in many places other than those already covered by the current free postage, we hope this will be implemented in time.

Please do visit us and get the feel of the website, many read us for months before building up the courage to post.... please don't leave it too long as we are very welcoming." Teresa Theobald (Army Mum)

Free parcel post   www.parcels43.co.uk

PHONE CALLS

You phoning them or them phoning you are brilliant ways to keep in touch. A very special way to "meet". Every little word is a treasure no matter what you happily or lovingly chat about. You wish the calls could be longer and longer but unfortunately they can't be which is rather disappointing. All you can do is make the most of what you get. However, you do get used to short calls and learn many ways to pack in as much as possible in short spaces of time. You will enjoy it from start to finish filling it with lots of stuff you have been itching to tell them and vice versa. Say lots of "I love you" and "I miss you" intermingled. Make the conversation enjoyable and fun so that you are both as happy as Larry. Even when you hang up you can have sweet, comforting words flowing round in your head.

Try to keep a little note by the phone of special reminders you want to ask or tell him/her because it is so frustrating when you put the phone down and you want to kick yourself for not telling him/her a specific, seemingly vital piece of information.

Don't be grumpy if phone calls are few and not on a regular basis. "TIME" and opportunity can make it extremely difficult. Often the work shifts are so long that they barely get the time to eat or even get a couple of hours of very much needed sleep. So make allowances for this problem in all the situations from start to finish of this tour.

With the landline calls you may get cut off mid call so don't get your knickers in a twist should it happen. Calls are monitored and this happens when necessary. The mind can play tricks and you wonder if something awful has happened to them. Why oh why has that occurred? Wild imaginings surround you and take hold. You start wondering what the reason might be and again you are flooded with worry as if perhaps some drastic thing has happened to cut the phone off. Lists of possibilities buzz round your mind. Try to relax and convince yourself it is just one of those tiny but annoying things. One of the many blips that can grip you with allsorts of things randomly throughout the tour. Being cut off is a painful kick to your system and so you get all worked up. Sit down or go and make yourself a cuppa so you can cool down and breathe slowly and think about all the good things said even if it was cut off in such a rather swift, brutal and unpleasant fashion. It seems so unfair. Always hone in on the positives rather than negatives. Any sort of call is better than none at all. It is another section of your learning curve for you as you fly wildly upon this roller coaster.

Your soldier gets 30 free minutes phone card per week from the army. Lets face it you are bound to want to chat much more than that per week. There is a way that you can top up their phone card so that you can have more time to talk. By calling 01438 28 2121 enables you to do this. You will need their phone card number along with their rank and name and their army number.

Mobile phones can be used, including texting, but there are various problems with them, which isn't such a boon. Signals and connections can be very poor indeed. One little sand storm and no hope of getting through is a certainty. When I say poor I do not exaggerate at all. Dreadful sometimes although connections are improving. It is also a very expensive way to call. It might be beneficial to find out the exact cost. In some theatres of war they are not allowed at all. A pain in the butt for sure but rules are rules and for reasons you cannot see immediately. In some areas they are not even allowed to take mobiles on tour with them. They are totally banned.

The reason they are banned is for safety. If they are out on an operation or off camp they need to try and stay as hidden as possible from the enemy. The phone gives away their location from the signal it emits so that the enemy know exactly where to train their missiles, rockets, bombs and mortars. Nobody wants that unhealthy situation to occur. The danger is immense. It only takes one stupid and irresponsible soldier breaking this rule because they think they are being clever so that they can use their phone when at the front line. It risks the lives of every soldier with them. It is truly evil and all because they want to chat with family or friends. Please don't encourage it despite the fact you will have to go a while without hearing anything when they are on ops. It's very hard to be without contact but war situations prove difficult to cope with and time and place determines whether phoning is possible. You must adhere to and accept it. Safety is number 1 in my eyes and I am sure you feel the same.

CARE WITH PHONECALL CHAT

When you talk on the phone there are certain things that should not be said over the lines just in case any of the baddies are picking up the conversation. Yes, they have the technology for them to do it both on landline and mobile phones. The landline phones are monitored so will cut out if you are careless. Truly this monitoring can seem such a nuisance but it is for safety. Don't be distressed by it. One thing to smile about is that the rules on the learning curve certainly have their purpose and all to make things better. Another smile to know your darling is in the safest of hands.

Do not speak of army dates or chat about events that have happened or are about to happen re the troops.

No talk about how the Forces are coping and if they are at a low ebb about something or of plans they may be considering.

Do not mention Rank or surnames and certainly not your address or anyone else's.

Do not mention personal phone numbers or e-mail addresses.

No political chat.

When it comes to giving you dates for R&R or final return home at the end of tour then it should be put in a letter or in e-mail. We don't want to let the enemy know of any movements of flight. By following these rules you are helping greatly.

When your soldier joined up he/she took an oath to restrict a great deal of information. This also means to friends and family so don't try and draw it out. Don't have him/her break that oath just because you are nosey. You have to respect that side of all of the Forces. You will be told things during their time from joining up but only on a need to know basis and not more.

PHONING CUDDLES

There will be times when you need a cuddle and vice versa. However when your soldier phones they may really need an extra something. An extra boost to their morale. They perhaps seem a bit down and detached from the conversation. This is because they miss us and are having a bad day or a bad week from situations out there. They can experience horrific sights and sounds that can be really testing them to the core. It can be so profound that we can't imagine their deep trauma. They have called to hear your voice so that you can pick up their spirits and to remind them that, yes you do love them and miss them as much as they do you. They haven't called to torment us with their feelings of insecurity. They have called because they know we can convey huge hugs and they are desperate to get a phone call cuddle from the person they know loves them and you can make it happen. A lot of gentleness and understanding will be needed to quench their thirst for reassurance and any doubts. It's a far cry from the real thing but a cuddle nonetheless. You can make everything seem a bit more okay and leave them feeling a little lighter and less stressed. They too are on an emotional roller coaster of their own and like us are experiencing all of the ups and downs but they handle things differently. There will be many times that you will need cuddles of reassurance in exactly the same way. However, the hearing of each others voices of comforting words, for as long as the conversation lasts, puts a smile like there's no tomorrow onto both of your faces. Closeness even at a distance is so important. During your separation you have to become expert in boosting up his/her morale, which in turn gives you a buzz with that very special and loving achievement. It is a huge struggle but you will learn different ways to have those calls contain the cure for emotional needs. Verbal hugs and cuddles and many noisy blown kisses are so important and will come naturally to you.

After the call do not get worried if your feelings are a mix so not only do you get a huge zip of elation from it you may experience being very upset afterwards too. It is a very common reaction after any call. It happens after the best and happiest of calls. A fantastic high with a boost of morale that is inexplicable and then a while later, because you now wish the call could have gone on non-stop, is when deflation overwhelms you. However you are always ready to make ordinary phone calls into extra special ones once you get the knack of the best way that suits you both. Even if it can cause lots of tears after a real high you know it's just a temporary feeling and very much worth it for the superb feeling to warm you inside.

USING YOUR COMPUTER

If you have a computer then it really is worth its weight in gold. If you haven't got one then think seriously about getting one. Unfortunately they are expensive so instead you could use the computer in the library. The librarians will be only too happy to show you how to use their ones. Going to an Internet Café is another good alternative. You may be able to use a friends one. A computer can be used in so many ways to help to get you through this trying TIME. This enables you to have special contact as well as find army chat sites so that you can contact others in the same boat as you. They are people who understand your plight because it is their plight too. Who better to chat with as these people? Understanding at your fingertips.

You can use it to send e-mails. Takes your breath away when you check it out and see in your Inbox that one or more are in it for you. It can put your blood pressure up high just to see that it is there before you have even read it. Being a Mum I got brilliant ones but rather short. Just a few sentences long but even though they were small they meant the world to me. They put me on cloud 9. Lengthwise didn't matter because at least it meant that I knew from each one how my son was and how life was treating him. His ups and downs. His highs and lows and believe it or not some funny situations that made me laugh. I don't know how other Mums would accept this reduced communication but in my case it didn't bother me at all. The apron strings once cut have to allow sons and daughters to blossom out into their own way of life. It may sound a bit naff though because as a Mum one always thinks of your matured children still as their youngsters no matter what their age. Unless you are a parent you wont understand that. Deep down in your heart that is how it seems to feel for me at any rate. If you disagree then maybe it is because I am weird haha! My e-mails to him were so long and so frequent I think he had to have matchsticks at the ready and a huge mug of coffee to keep him awake when trying to read the epistles.

My sons very lengthy ones that he wrote went to his fiancé. That is just as it should be. I don't think she would have been very understanding if hers were short like mine. In actual fact I reckon she would have been fuming mad and heartbroken if his e-mails were on the skimpy side. Rightly, hers were far from short. She was overjoyed and floating on air with each one that she received and all the ones that she sent.

All camps have computers. As you can imagine they are not state of the art with them being used so often by so many! They are slightly over used, to put it politely, but they work pretty well all things considered. Sometimes soldiers have to book a time slot to use them as they are in great demand or they can take potluck that one is free. Pray that the latter is how it will mainly be. Hope deeply and dream that there might be times when it can be used when nobody else wants to use it. You will soon find out that the time may be at some unearthly hour due to time zones or their ability to fit it in when they finish a work shift. This is a huge determining factor that could mean it will be at various times and not on a regular basis. Get an alarm clock set to wake you if it's halfway through the night. It's not ideal but well worth breaking up your nights sleep. Everything is worth waiting for at any time even if you are yawning your head off. I am sure you will agree on that. Nothing is simple or straightforward as by now you will have realised.

INSTANT MESSENGER

This is an ideal way to keep in touch. It is probably one of the best ways to being as close and interactive as possible with your loved one. Yack away to your hearts content about anything and everything. OK it's not "never ending" but time lengths can be very long indeed. Woohooo. So fingers, eyes and legs crossed that it will be just right (do not do that when typing or you will hit the wrong keys) You may find transmitting time could be a touch slow in sending and receiving the messages of your chat which although frustrating is also a giggle because you will most certainly realise that heavens you are sure you are not that slow at typing compared with normal and previous conversations. It all depends upon the condition of their computer. The extra thing you can do is read the chat that you had several times over.

Using Messenger will be a huge bonus to chat with any friends you make along this roller coaster ride. Like-minded people who understand and each can comfort you and vice versa.

THE EBLUEY SITE

Sending e-blueys are a fantastic boon. You are very likely to send loads of them. They are a type of electronic letter that can only be used for the Forces.

Sending an e-bluey, (Electronic bluey) which is the real reason for this site, is a speedy way to send a special e-mail used for people at a BFPO address and it stays totally confidential. The army receives what you send and with the use of an integrated mail printer that prints it out in letterform and a machine seals it automatically so nobody can read it at any stage. This is available wherever they are worldwide. It is taken to the soldier in letterform whether they are out in the field or on camp within 12 to 36 hours. Usually it can be just a matter of hours if you are extremely lucky. It is such a popular way to keep in contact that I know you will probably use the site daily. Improvements to the system are being made all the time. Updates can be found at the BFPO website.

If you wish you can send a photo ebluey. This is the facility to have a photo printed on it too. How cool is that? They are very high quality so no doubt you will send that type from time to time.

On very rare occasions, which I doubt you will ever experience, when eblueys cannot be downloaded in the theatre of operations they are destined for, they are downloaded and printed in BFPO London depot and then forwarded by Airmail.

OTHER EBLUEY SITE USES

At another section of this site there is a place where you can post messages on the board called Support The Troops Messages to send your soldier love. At some camps the page gets printed out so that every soldier can check to see if there is a message posted from home. You will find it is fun to read the other messages posted. Who isn't nosey? Very few of us. I am a really nosey breed and cannot resist! I poured over it a lot. Admit it you can't stop yourself either to read tons of them out of interest, plus it is also comforting to know that there are people out there that feel the same way you do and show their soldier as much love as you do yours. In every way you are getting into the swing of using all ways and means that you can find to give you as many possibilities available at your fingertips.

EBLUEY CHATBOARD

What a fantastic section this is without a doubt. It is a message board for you to post messages that can be shared by other people just like you. They too have the same weird and highly emotional problems so you can understand each other right from the start. It is a true lifeline for you to use and get huge benefits. This is such a friendly place where you will feel that you are part of one huge family. So, there is absolutely no reason to be worried about posting. People of all ages and in different situations on it whether you are family or friends of anybody of the Forces in Iraq or Afghanistan. It is ideal to swap information or have general happy chitchat on what your day has been like etc. As well as you getting help you will find that you too can help others. Everyone moulds together by learning information and giving out information between you. You can support each other through thick and thin. You can laugh, moan and cry together. Tell your tales of woe and happiness and discuss and chew over just about everything. No question is too big or small because amongst you there is bound to be somebody who can answer your queries. There will be ways for you to advise others. It's a massive learning curve of varied hugs, fun and comfort. You will make many friends on there. I did. If you are having a bit of a rough day then people can help you using their own similar experiences and vice versa. Togetherness is a big comfort blanket of group hugs. When you get an e or other contact from your soldier the board rings with happiness when you mention it. You bounce off each other's feelings. It really cheers you up. In fact it does have one rather large problem that goes with it though. HEALTH WARNING. THIS BOARD IS HIGHLY ADDICTIVE WITH NO KNOWN

CURE!

The board is carefully monitored so that any unsavoury messages will be deleted before being posted. You are allowed to put your own e-mail address on so that people can e you and you can e others. Many friendships will be forged. The great thing will be getting to know people who you can talk to either on Messenger or even on the telephone. People who are having all the same problems you have so that you can relate to each other. They are terrific support to you and equally you to them. You never know you may get to meet up with the ones who live close to you for girlie days or nights out. There are bound to be military chat sites that other's know of so they can be a real boon.

Certain things will not be allowed. No dates, numbers, phone numbers or urls. No swearing. Try to be respectful to others. If you put on any of those then they will show up as xxx in their place.

A chat board is not a place to scaremonger or harass. You don't want to panic people any more than likewise you don't want to be panicked or frightened. You may find rumours are rife at times so remember that information can be wrong, exaggerated, half truths and a bit like Chinese whispers which are so way off the mark. Don't think that because a person says that such and such is happening or going to happen that it refers to your loved one being affected in a situation that could be similar. Ignore things like that or you will get upset and you certainly don't want to be worried over nothing. Keep your mind wide-open and put things in perspective. You have to accept that the board will be a mix of many different people with a range of ages and outlooks who has a family member or friend deployed and some of whom might be more highly strung than others. The board is for happy chat and support and not for scary and rubbish ideas that are not substantiated. Don't go bananas on a mention of such things. You have to learn to keep your cool. But I promise you that the ebluey site will get you through and boost you up. I remain on it to welcome and try to help with the queries that I am able to answer even when my son isn't on a deployment. Come to the board and see what you think. It will be a lifesaver for you.

Have you ever considered making your own chat-room? Perhaps you and a couple of others could decide to do it then any of you can pop in and out as you please. You could let the friends on the ebluey to join in and use it. I have had a chat-room for years and decided to use it with similar people in the same boat as me. Part of the interesting time filler is searching for good sites.

If you go to www.yellowribbon.org.uk you will find that a friendly site to go into its chat-room and use the forums and other links and sections. You may even get involved with charity work they do.

www.ukmilitaryfamilies.bravehost.com This is an ideal site to join as its got allsorts to help everyone like us.

www.Armywivesunited.co.uk/ Although this name says wives it is for any female be they relatives or friends of a soldier. Really they are so friendly and welcoming that you will fit in straight away. There are so many different sections of it to go to. The choices are enormous. One peep and you will be hooked on it.

www.army.co.uk That is good for all types of army stuff

www.helpforheroes.org.uk Help For Heroes. That is a lovely charity that works hard to support our wounded. You can donate or buy various objects. I always wear their wristband. Have you noticed that Princes William and Harry wear them? I have a sticker on the car. I have a mug and a Mouse mat. The cartoon pictures of our wounded troops can only make you laugh, as they are so amusing. Something that is humorous from something serious. You can get notepads, ties and socks all with their logo on.

Look up on website:

Soldier Magazine   You can also get their monthly magazine

AFF Journal (Army Families Federation) They do a 3 monthly magazine

They are all highly recommended and easily available for you.

Other readable things to help you are NEWSLETTERS.

There are camp monthly NEWSLETTERS and packages given out to forces families then if you decide you would like them too just contact the Families Welfare Officer at your soldier's barracks and they will organise it so that you too can have a copy sent. They will put you on their database. It will keep you updated on many things. It also tells you of any outings and meetings arranged that you could participate in.

You may find it advantageous to chat through any other problems you may need help or advice with at the same time. Your Army Families Welfare officer is a Godsend. They are a good port of call for lots of problems.

PARADIGM

Look up Paradigm to help you with your communications. There is a family services page where it gives you all the information for topping up phone cards.

WelComE telephone and Internet The WelComE (Welfare Communications Everywhere) service is provided by Paradigm as part of the Skynet 5 PFI contract with the MoD. Paradigm has provided over a million hours of welfare telephone calls since Op Telic began and provides Internet and email services, that are free for use to entitled UK military personnel deployed on operations overseas. **Family and friends information** Family and friends can leave free voicemail messages and top-up the Paradigm account cards of entitled UK military personnel currently serving on operational duty overseas. Please ensure that you use the correct phone numbers provided. **Top-up service** Paradigm will need the following information from you:

- Their name and rank

- Their 9-digit Paradigm account card number

- Your own debit/credit card details **Free voicemail service (UK)** You will need to:

    - Dial 0800 051 0737 (freephone number when calling from a UK landline only)

    - At voice prompt, enter the 9-digit Paradigm account card number of the person to whom you

wish to leave a message
- Leave your message
- Hang up

Messages can last up to 2 minutes A maximum of 10 messages can be saved per account Voicemails can be saved for a maximum of 60 days only Free message retrieval service for in-theatre contact Network extras may apply, Please contact your telephone provider for details. For further details, please contact: The WelComE Customer Contact Centre

Opening hours: (UK) Mon – Fri 0600hrs to 2200hrs

Telephone: 01438 282121

E-mail: customersupport@paradigmservices.com

Paradigm had already established itself as a service provider through WELCOME (WELfare COMmunications Everywhere – a welfare communications service for the UK MOD), successfully providing Voice, E-mail and Internet services to UK Armed Forces serving on operational duty overseas. This contract now forms part of the wider Skynet 5 remit.

Paradigm is under contract to the UK MOD for the Skynet 5 programme.

THE HOME PAGE POSTAL BEARS

On the ebluey site home page it advertises different types of Postal bears with 74 regimental teddies to choose from. Every Regiment, rank and job is catered for. There is the choice as to them being either in ordinary uniform or desert combats. It can help you and the children imagine just what your soldier looks like. A very cute and cuddly reminder indeed. It is a lovely section to browse through even if you don't buy one. It will brighten you up just to look. I have one and he sits proudly on the settee. I don't take mine to bed with me though you may well decide to. They are perfect in every detail. They are meant for family or friends at home although some people do send them to their soldier. So I suggest you look through and decide for yourself if it is a desirable teddy for you. I am sure you will find similar teddies at many other places. It's all a case of hunt and see. www.postalbears.co.uk

On the home page there is a shop advertised with all types of wonderful things and gifts for all people and for all occasions. They vary in price from cheap, medium or downright expensive. So it is suitable for anyone's pocket. Its fun to search through every type even if the majority of people cannot buy the very costly items which may make you suck your teeth like I did by seeing the price tag and wondered just who can afford them. It makes one dream the " what if I could buy the out of reach items?" type of dream! Then you spring back to reality and your dream is shattered. Never mind it was only a dream of wishful thinking. It was quite nice while it lasted though. Back to looking at my price range was the sensible route to take.

I know there are countless shops that you will probably find somewhere like it so I advise you search about. It perhaps could be time-consuming fun therapy for you to do that.

BOXHAPPY

Are you a bit stuck for sending a special gift parcel? Then go to boxhappy.com. Just check it out. Perhaps a problem is solved. You can buy their various parcels via the net with Boxhappy. There are countless choices of contents. It may give you some ideas to put in your parcels even if you don't use BOXHAPPY. Have a look at this option and you will see what I mean. It is a site you and your soldier might use. They are beautifully wrapped parcels and you choose a card to go inside it. A short cut to go to this site is to click on the little icon of a file next to your soldier's name in your ebluey site address book. It takes you automatically to it.

THE FORCES RADIO STATION

There is BFBS (British Forces Broadcasting Service) It is available on Sky TV radio channel 0211. Stations in Iraq & Afghanistan and Germany are joining with BFBS UK to maintain a 24hr a day service with daily, live programmes from the very heart of operational areas where our troops are based. Hear what's happening in Iraq and Afghanistan. Enjoy the music.

This is where you can post dedications/messages for Birthdays, Anniversaries or for absolutely no reason at all but as a sweet way for you to spread your love by this radio station that the troops listen to most of the time. You choose the date. Your request will be read out during the regular broadcasting. What a way to show how much you miss them. You are going to have a fantastic feeling of elation as you listen to each word. It will be a surge of lovey dovey cuddly stuff. While on cloud 9 and he/she will be there with you glowing inside too. You will feel a fantastic buzzing surge inside. A miniscule few may be a bit ragged by their mates! I am sure this probably is caused by a touch of envy because the message isn't for them. A bit of leg pulling is par for the course. You can be sure the boost up of your loved ones morale will be very worthwhile. It is a way of letting everyone know your feelings and for sure you want everybody possible to hear it.

Here is a letter I got from a lady called Daisy who says exactly what happened to her. (o/h is a shortened term used in chat rooms/boards meaning Other Half)

"I have thought about the two occasions I have posted requests using the bfbs website. On both occasions I was unsure what time to select for the request to be played as I was unsure whether is was meant to be UK time or Afghan time - subsequently both requests were not heard by my o/h but other soldiers did tell him about them. The last time I put a request in for our anniversary and despite selecting June 2nd for the request to be read-out it was actually read the day before which I thought was strange when they particularly ask you what date you'd like it reading out and what occasion it is for.

Those are my thoughts. I know my o/h was pretty disappointed that he missed both of the requests but was glad that I'd made the effort and was thinking about him. So it definitely cheered him up and improved his morale."

That was Daisy's example. Nothing is guaranteed to be exact every time but its well worth a try to get that fantastic ripple through you both. As Daisy says they accidentally got the dates wrong in her case but they were both over the moon despite that.Call 08701 202121 (calls cost 8p per min from BT landline, other networks may vary.

Email: access@bfbs.com

Text: 07740 377 377 start text with AAA

www.bfbs.com/digital

FRIENDS DON'T UNDERSTAND ME

You had it all sorted out in your head before the tour began. You have plenty of friends and family to help you. Wait a moment because what you planned and what is happening doesn't seem to match up at all. They start to think that you really are taking it all a great deal more extreme to the way they imagined too. To them it doesn't relate at all. Yes, they are fine for a shoulder to cry on and give you a certain amount of support but where are they with all this comfort when you and them realise it isn't just a case of being low or down. You are so low your heart is in your boots and life is way out of control. Your behaviour is scary and nothing like expected. They had assumed it was going to be a situation to cope with. Ready to help you at miserable times and never considered it to be the heightened way it becomes. They assume it will be now and again but not constant. You might even scare them off because they are at a total loss to comfort you the way you need. They might have assumed that after a couple of weeks the sadness would have worn off. It doesn't though does it. It goes on and on and on. Every day until the end of the tour it is with you. There will be a lot of times friends and family will jump down your throat and angrily and unsympathetically say for you to "Pull yourself together" as if you can turn it off like a tap. Nobody who is depressed can do that at all. Oh my, why are they being like this? Your plan never worked out for you or them which is so sad. A shock to the system for them seeing you being unbelievably and inconsolably shocked. You feel somewhat abandoned as well as kicked in the teeth. There is a massive hole inside of you that in no way can be helped. Your reckoning is so off the mark. How rotten for you. Even if you go out with friends you might feel like the odd man out. You can feel alone even in a crowd. They are worried that you are going to be an ace pain in the butt at some point, if not all the time you are out. Sarcasm and criticism will spit forth from you to them and back again. Tetchiness runs through the time out so that all of what should have been a fun night or group get together is a big disaster for each of you in some way. It isn't going to be bad every time and it is good to go out often but do be prepared for things to go a touch rough for your feelings to cope with. Just hope of hopes there is somebody who can still be your support and guardian angel to stick with you from beginning to the end of the tour. This doesn't mean you lose your friends but just have some space at this time if you feel it would be best. It wont happen to you all but for a lot of people like you they can't be of a great help for that pain they can't get a grip of. Your mood swings can be so bad and so often. Sudden explosions from nowhere.

This situation of misunderstanding, I call it the "Broken Limb Syndrome". Compare it to trying to console someone who has a broken leg or arm. The plaster cast can be seen. That is more than evident but a person consoling them can't feel the pain underneath or even guess at it unless they too have had a similar injury. It is the same with you and your pain that is causing your life to be unbearable at times. People know your situation but that pain inside they can't feel. They have no idea and nothing to compare it to. That is why I say that mixing with people just like yourself is your best bet. You understand each other's problems and difficulties. You understand each other's hurts and heartbreaks. The identical highs and lows. They will also have sleepless nights like you so you can both natter at all hours because your normal friends wont want to be up through the night nattering away to you when they would prefer to be curled up fast asleep.

It might be beneficial for you to let a friend or two of your ordinary friends to borrow this book so that they can possibly understand you a little bit better. It might improve the situation. I can't guarantee it will but there is no harm in trying to get a better effect. The togetherness can be a vital bond in order to win through this difficult time.

There is all the shallow patronising talk that really can make you annoyed. The "Don't worry, everything will be ok" type of chat that sounds rather false and you would prefer your friends didn't keep on saying that so very many times. You know they are saying it in the hope it will cheer you up. You know it is a verbal cuddle so don't dismiss it as your family and friends do want to help you any way they can. They are bound to tread on a few toes and vice versa. They are going to need cuddles from you. You cannot always be the one comforted because some of them are as ripped up as much as you. Therefore cuddles for them too. Don't feel sorry for yourself as if you are the only one feeling bad. Becoming self-centred can be an easy direction to slip into without realising it.

FILL UP YOUR TIME

There are lots of ways to fill up your time. More things possible than you would have even thought up. It is such a difficult subject to touch upon because we all prefer to enjoy or hook onto our individual choices so only you can choose what's the best. Filling up your spare time is good because free time becomes thinking time where your mind departs in so many directions resulting in the use of those tissues again. Nobody wants the blotchy face; red eyes and looking a ghastly mess becoming fashionable for you. These results from worrying must be kept to a minimum where it is at all possible. Keeping your days full can make your life so much easier. Being engrossed in something is the answer.

Here are some ideas that you can sift through to add to your own ideas. Some of these can involve you doing them with friends or family. Most of them you will be doing alone. Other more difficult things may turn out really naff but it mustn't bother you at all as its all part of this vast rich pattern of your learning curve. Have a go no matter what the final result is. Believe in yourself. Get stuck in. Contact Family Welfare to see if they have certain things planned to do. Take the plunge and go because you will make a lot of friends who are like you, while enjoying yourself at the same time. It could be lovely trips out or doing other arranged things to be part of. Join in.

Here are some ideas for you to be active or get engrossed in.

READ

Snuggling up with a good book and a cuppa can be done at anytime of the day or night. Whether its while you are relaxing on the sofa or half under the bedclothes to help you off to sleep. Go to the library and you can't go wrong for choice of books. Root amongst the second hand book stalls and charity shops to see if there are any that might be just the sort for you.

Be sure to stay away from war books. They are definitely not on the list.

WATCH TV and VIDEOS

You are bound to have lots of favourite programmes that you have always watched so plan out your evenings viewing. Soaps, Dramas, Quiz Shows, comedians that can really give you sniggers and giggles or educational programmes on Sky Discovery to expand your little grey cells. This is your special time to dig out videos you haven't looked at in years and are now a little covered in dust or go and hire a few.

PLAY COMPUTER GAMES

Play fun ones that make you smile and feel all bright inside. There are hundreds to choose from and they can be a way to fill up hours without you realising it.

PUZZLE BOOKS

There are lots of ones to get. Various brainteasers, Word searches etc. I found those giant crossword books are very good. I have to admit that Coffee Time ones are my forte as I never found the Cryptic ones in my league at all. They were truly over my head when it came to looking at them let alone attempting one.

JIGSAWS

Do not do overly large or impossible ones or you will get so angry and fed up that you may find you are picking up pieces when thrown around the room. Always settle for a medium type of puzzle unless of course you are expert at them. (I wish!)

ARTS AND CRAFTS

All towns have a craft shop so pop in and see if anything takes your fancy. It could be painting by numbers. Embroidering pictures. Model making. Candle making. Make your own mug kits. The world is your oyster in there. I doubt if you will come out empty handed. OK you may think it will turn out gross and be an ace disaster but it doesn't matter. So what if it does, because at least you will have enjoyed doing it and it will have kept you very busy. You will have tried to do something that you have never done before. It might turn out first class. Be proud of it no matter what the result is. Never let your lack of confidence say " I can't try that" It is something that everyone has to do for the first time. The perfect things to have a go at.

START A COURSE AT COLLEGE

The selection is immense with things you can do at night school. There are many types which you probably never got the chance trying to do although in the back of your mind you have always thought it could be good to do. As a starting point go to the local college or University and get some pamphlets on what is available. The local library may be able to give you some information about it. It may just give you the extra push to decide on doing something. Many friendships will be made in whatever course you choose.

FLOWER ARRANGING

Go to night classes for it or get a teach-yourself manual. It is an unusual hobby but so enjoyable and heaps of satisfaction and fun.

TAKE PHOTOS

Practice lots and have a happy time snapping away at anything and everything you see. You will learn by your mistakes but there will be many of them you can send off in your parcel and feel pleased about. I am sure he/she will love getting them even if they are a bit wonky or with heads slightly chopped off. Some good ones you could use as screen savers. Others use to make up notelettes and greetings cards and collages. Always frame the best and put them well displayed for not only you to see but for anyone who comes to the house so they will catch their eye upon them too. Digging out old photos and making up a scrapbook might be interesting or make a scrapbook of all the new things you have taken. Take photos really close up of minuscule parts of items that your soldier would normally see around the home. Send them to him/her to guess what they are. Don't make it too easy for them and do it so they really have to ponder a very long while even if it takes days to perhaps eventually have an inkling as to what the object might be.

A DUVET DAY

Once in a while enjoy a "Duvet Day" when you stay in your PJ's. Don't put make-up on. Snuggle up on the settee with a fleecy blanket, a cup of hot chocolate, comfort food and watch trash TV or a film. Perhaps read and do puzzles. You do whatever you fancy that keeps you like a couch potato. Don't answer the door. Just wallow. This is your special day when you can laze around and do nothing or something non energetic and which is totally different from the normal type of day.

COOKERY AND DANCING CLASSES

These are brilliant if you get a few of your friends together. Line dancing, Country dancing, Ballroom or Pop. If not then go alone and you are bound to quickly make some friends. With the cookery you might go to classes and/or experiment with things you have never tried to do before so get a good "learn to cook /recipe book". Use herbs and foods that are totally new to you. Watch cookery programmes on TV and make notes of hints and tips. I wish you the very best of luck on that one. Your cupboards and fridge can be full of lovely surprises when your soldier returns for r&r or for the end of the tour. That's when you can amaze him/her with your culinary skills.

THE GYM

Go and have a look around at your sports/health/leisure centre to see if there is anything that might be just what you fancy. Aerobics, keep fit, bodybuilding, various sports like badminton or tennis. Perhaps learn to swim if you can't or just enjoy the pool if you can. Learn to dive a bit better than those belly flops that you are only capable of doing. Pamper yourself with a sauna. You could probably go with a friend on a regular basis to make the most of all there is. Take the kids. All this exercise will help you to sleep at nights. You wont need rocking and neither will the children.

JOGGING

It may sound awesome to think about it but start off with short distances and expand on your distance gradually. Do not forget to take a camera with you because you are bound to see places and views you never thought existed. You could go jogging in the woods, countryside, town, park or beach. It doesn't have to be anywhere special. Wherever you go the fresh air will do you good and make you feel much brighter. Expand your lungs.

CYCLING

Cycling you may prefer to do with a friend or your children. If you have a job and it isn't too far away then think about biking to work. Maybe there will be days when you won't be so enamoured if the weather is too nasty but anytime is better than none.

YOGA CLASSES

This is a good relaxation technique that could iron out a lot of your tension both muscular and mental. Then again you may get into knottier problems! Try it and see. This is something you can practice and use at home.

RELAXATION CLASSES

Learning to relax can help you when you are really feeling uptight on very down days. Breathing techniques and other similar abilities can be a good way with coping. Meditation is possibly for you.

However if you are very depressed or sleeping badly then do not hesitate in seeing your doctor who may prescribe a helpful medication. In some cases a therapist could be the answer to un-bottle all of your troubles. A problem shared is a problem halved. You really should seek expert advice and not struggle on trying to fix things all by yourself. You will find that your doctor will select what is right for you. Friends tend to tell you that they have the solution to your depression without seeking medical help but everyone is different. Some friends suggestions might be good for them and in no way right for you. Being in tune with yourself is essential. You are such an important person so don't disregard or neglect the "YOU". Treasure the "YOU".

KEEP FIT VIDEOS

I am sure you will find one that is right for you. Don't forget your soldier won't be there to laugh at you learning. It can be so off putting at first when there is someone who tells you what an idiot you look. You can dance about and get in the strangest positions while loudly singing. Try not to disturb the neighbours! However do take heart and persevere because your soldier will be over the moon when the results are seen. Focus and be determined. Don't give up at the first hurdle or when some twinges or muscle aches start to put you off. Enjoy.

SLIMMING

Putting on weight can easily happen with all the comfort snacking you do. You could join a slimming club and hopefully watch those unwanted pounds disappear. You can be more inspired if you do it that way as a group. You might prefer to find a good food regime that you can stick to at home. I am sure you have a friend or relative who can advise you of a good diet that worked for them. Once again no pointy fingers from your soldier if at times you lapse a little. No nagging, criticising or laughing you down if it fails. You do it your way and at your rate. You might consider becoming a vegetarian though I don't know if your soldier will be too enamoured with that if he/she loves meat. Maybe you should warn him first as we don't want to upset him/her with too many changes. Only you can decide upon that. Be sure you have good scales to check on your weight occasionally but don't use them too much. Once a week is better.

LEARN A LANGUAGE

There must have been times when you wished you could speak another language. Not for only the ability to do so but to put it to use when you go on your holidays. That will really make you puff out your chest with pride. Go to an evening class to learn. You may prefer to get one of those handy learn at home language kits and be sure to put aside a time each day to do it. You may end up doing your housework while listening to it. You might even get addicted as well. It will be very rewarding.

JOB RETRAINING

Is your present job getting you down? Perhaps doing a new one may be needed. Another place with the same job could make you feel fresher. You can retrain for a different type of job. They say a change is as good as a rest. Also if you haven't got a job perhaps it could help if you did get one. Anything that can get you out from 4 walls is beneficial.

LEARN TO DRIVE

Now is the opportunity to take lessons. You could have said on lots of occasions that you will learn but you have always seemed to put it off for no apparent reason. You now have no excuse. The actual learning is fun and it gives you a mark on your calendar for each of your lessons. The freedom it will give you once you have passed will be immeasurable. You can then be so proud of yourself for a big achievement.

FAMILY TREE AND IT'S HISTORY

Have you ever thought about doing one? It will take a lot of searching and digging out information from your relatives but I can assure you it wont be an easy thing to do but very interesting and satisfying. Some family members will know bits that another doesn't know. You could even do a lot of searching on the Internet. It really is fascinating going through your ancestry. I managed to get back into the 1700's. Doing one requires a lot of patience and a lot of head scratching. A great deal of tearing your hair out when you become stuck.

FRIENDS REUNITED

Perhaps a good old get together with school pals could be something nice. Updating each other of things since schooldays. A brilliant way to do it is by going to Friends Reunited on your computer where it has every school, university and work place sections. www.friendsreunited.co.uk A real place to hunt around. Find yours and see how many classmates are on it for your years. You could end up getting in touch with people you had forgotten existed as a lot of memories of school do fade away. I have to admit that I find it intriguing, a good laugh and jolly good fun by contacting and staying in contact with long lost friends. Organising a reunion is a good idea.

There is a section of it called Genes Reunited too that will help you with your Family Tree.

A section for military

One for work mates

So many different sections for finding others. Friends Reunited is a popular and well-used place to go to.

GIRLIE NIGHTS OUT OR IN

Its always good for you to go out for the evening with friends and family so that you can all have a little bit of freedom or something to focus on. You mustn't stay in and vegetate. It could be for a dinner in a restaurant. You could go to a pub or club. A possible meet up in a coffee bar is the answer. Off to the cinema. Do whatever is to your taste. In some cases finding a babysitter isn't at all easy. This could be where your Mum or Dad will be only too willing to do it. At times a close friend or neighbour could be your saviour. Girlie nights in may be better where you cook a meal and lounge in front of the TV with snacks and watch your favourite programmes or get a video or two. You could have a really good natter. You could take it in turns as to whose house you go to each time. You could go out for the day and take a picnic with you. A bunch of ladies together can be fantastic if you use your imagination. Remember to try out your newly learned recipes.

HAVE AN ANNE SUMMERS PARTY

This can be a real hoot getting all the sexy undies. You will be like silly schoolgirls together being as daft as you want to and perhaps spending a little more than you should. Don't forget you are doing it not just for you but also for your man when he comes back so he can't really complain.

HAVE A SHOPPING SPREE ALONE OR WITH FRIENDS

Take a bus or train away from your usual town to a place you haven't been to before and either window shop or buy. Try on all types of both pretty and ugly clothes which is a giggle. It can be a super time without breaking your bank balance if it's window-shopping. If you have children then they will love it just as much as you do.

HELP A CHARITY

You may decide to do voluntary work for any charity. Contact a couple of them and spend free time helping one of your choice by selling items e.g. wristbands and badges or working in one of their shops. Do coffee mornings. This will not only be good for your ego but at the same time you will be helping so many others. All charities are desperate for volunteers.

You will do very well by asking your friends and workmates to donate to various military charities. People are only too happy to reach into their pocket to do so.

You may even be very brave enough to tackle a sponsored walk, bungi jump or parachute jump. Here I have to admit I am not that brave to attempt it.

PLAN A HOLIDAY

It isn't easy to do but the thinking about it and looking at tons of brochures from the Travel Agents can boost you up so much so that you get to the stage when having discussed it with your soldier you jump in at the deep end and sort things out for real. Send brochures for him/her to look at. Chew the ideas over when you contact. All the plus and minus sides to it. Look at the prices of flights by different airlines. You may not be going until the following year but it is all an extra brick to sorting out another huge but delicious item. You may not even be going on it at all but it's a bubbly thought. The entire fabric of your imaginations can give both of you a high when you chat about it together. Perhaps you have a Honeymoon to organise. An ideal time to search for a place where you might go.

WEDDING PLANS

You may have had the date set and there are all the arrangements to make. Even if it's a long way off it is superb to get into the flow of all the necessary fields to put your mind on course for it. Discuss it with both sides of the family. They may like to go on a bridal day out with you to look at the possibilities. You will have a brilliant time. Go to bridal shops and get all the bumf they have. Get two lots of bumf so that one set can be sent to him/her. The types of dresses for bride and bridesmaids, the suits, the cakes, bouquets, the invitation cards etc. Everything you can think of. That way you both have a say in each other's preferences. He/she may be far away but working it out can still go on. Not forgetting the vital thing called cost! Do lots of planning in your head and make lots of lists.

GARDENING

You may never have planted anything in your life but now is a good time to learn. Up until now all you might have done is sit back and enjoy the glorious blooms and aromas made for you. There is the lawn to keep mown. How to use a Hover without causing yourself any bodily harm. The flowerbeds you need to weed so that you can plant the prettiest of flowers for the best display possible. Even if it is just a case of planting something in a tub, hanging basket or tomatoes in a Grow-bag then do so. Homegrown vegetables, Runner beans, Strawberries and Blackberries are yummy. If you don't have a garden then do some window boxes or a herb garden. If you are not too sure about how to do this gardening lark then I am sure friends and neighbours can advise you. If you drop into your local Garden Centre they will give excellent information and the best advice too.

If there are any really tough, heavy-duty tasks that you know you can't do then ask a friendly neighbour to step in and give you a hand. Never be too shy to ask such favours.

Putting up a bird table will encourage quite a few types of bird to visit. Hang up some nuts and seeds. A heart-warming site to see. Sending photos of your plants in different stages of their growth and cute ones of the birds is a good idea.

Get someone who could take a photo of you actually gardening with mud up to your elbows or you with the hose or watering can. What about a photo of you being more genteel whilst doing it. Which would he/she prefer? Both types I am sure.

D.I.Y

You can do it if you put your mind to it. It may make you shake your head in the uncertainty that you can't but as I have said earlier you must have a go. Do not be daunted by any negativity, as you will make yourself proud to have taken on or attempted such tasks. I am sure that at times you have talked about doing this that and the other but have always only got as far as talking about it. Now those wont be only words but actions. By doing D.I.Y will make you feel much more independent and build up your confidence. There will be a lot to brag about. You will find it fun to go to the D.I.Y store and pick the paints and wallpaper. Don't rush though because you don't want to buy the wrong one or that would be a catastrophe from the word GO.

There must be a room or two that needs painting. Get a manual on how to do it or ask somebody you know to give you that first helping hand to get you started. Be very sure that carpets and furniture are well protected as you wont have on your wish list the splashes of paint that end up on those. Do not let children near any tins of paint or they might add to the décor, and that wouldn't be a too pretty. You do want your soldier on his/her return to be over the moon about what you have done. If all goes fine with one room then you may get addicted and do another.

Wallpapering is another way to brighten up the place. Again seek advice and if possible do it with a friend. It isn't as hard as you may think. Be brave and do the best. If it's a failure it doesn't matter.

You will see allsorts of little jobs that need to be done e.g. tiling and fitting new doorknobs. Cupboards to be brightened up. The whole DIY trip will keep your mind occupied daily for hours on end. There could be a shower to fit over the bath. The possibilities are endless. You will find lots of things to have a go at.

SPRING CLEAN

You could refresh the place by spring-cleaning and then with a bit of shifting of furniture or even throwing out the really yucky stuff that is overfilling your rooms. Make the place a bit more spacious. Get rid of items you never use or the many things you just keep for the sake of it. Don't be a hoarder. Blitz each room and be really strict so that you don't keep things that you consider may come in handy at sometime in the future or items "just in case". If you haven't used it for ages then there is no reason to still keep it. All it does is take up space that could be more wisely used for something new or useful. You could have it emptier to make things roomier and look ten times better. You will amaze yourself with the amount of rubbish you will throw out.

I WANT TO LOOK A REAL BEAUTY FOR MY MAN

You have such a long while to reach perfection so you can get it off to a fine art. Experiment with your hair colour and various styles until you find the one that looks the prettiest and sexiest looking. The one that makes you feel the most relaxed and happiest with. You don't want to look a wreck when you welcome your chap home. You need to look stunning for him. Be sure to make a hair appointment a day or two before he is due back.

Try a variety of different types of make-up. Don't rush into doing it because its good fun to try out all the ways possible for you to be adorable. It could be a giggle to do this with a friend. What woman doesn't want to dig into their make-up bags and do all the craziest ways possible as well as the most sensible and ideal?

Manicured nails are a definite YES. Firstly stop chewing them if you have that bad habit. Tut tut! Get them manicured at a parlour or do them yourself. Work on them a lot from day 1 to have them perfect. Spend lots of time on them. They need a lot of careful handling to get them tip-top. Get them so they are beautifully shaped. Eventually they are going to wow you as well as wow your man. Don't just change the colour of your nail varnish but how about doing some nail art. Patterns in painting them. It's great fun to do in every which way possible. You can get some nail gems and have a brilliant time seeing the ways that really make you say Coo! The gems are not expensive and have about 175 very pretty ones of different sizes, shapes and colours in the kit box. I tried it and got quite addicted to it although it can be a challenge as it is extremely fiddly to do. Fiddly it may be but at the same time gives immense satisfaction. You are bound to split your sides at times with some of the unexpected and unusual results.

Try pampering yourself by having a wax at a beauty parlour. Of course you can always do it yourself as either way it will look really special. Certain areas may be a bit painful although on the whole it isn't too bad at all so don't let painful stories put you off having a go. I am sure people only exaggerate on what it is truly like. One little tip here. Do not try it for the first time a few days before your man returns. For some unfortunates it can cause a bit of redness therefore it is best to see how your skin reacts and if it needs a certain number of days to settle back to its normal colour or that it is totally not an option for you. At least a trial run is beneficial.

What about a massage? A bit costly but it does loosen up all the tense muscles that you never even knew you had. Consider it as a little something you always wanted to try and now you are determined to do.

Body lotions, oils and creams are going to make your skin well toned up. Try out various shower gels. Use fake tan to look better and match your soldier who will come back very dark indeed.

With lots of window-shopping you are bound to come upon something new to wear for that very special day. Don't forget shoes to go with your outfit. It doesn't have to be costly or posh but relaxed and casual. Slacks and a jumper. Wear the type of thing you normally wear. Keep hunting and don't forget to slowly save up so that you can afford it, as you don't want to be suddenly paying out for it when you feel money might be a bit on the tight side.

By pampering yourself with some or all the suggestions will make you feel so much more confident inwardly and each time you look in the mirror you can enjoy and be chuffed with what you see. This also means that when you are amongst people, you will know that they will envy your beauty too. You can hold your head up high and stand proud that you have made them slightly envious. Pamper yourself to a greater or lesser degree. Be selective as to the things you will have a go at.

You are going to be the perfect picture to Wow your chap for sure the moment he sees your beauty. You are going to Wow him even if you haven't pampered yourself at all. Either way he will be over the moon to see you after so very long. The decision is yours.

NIGHT TIME

Those times can seem to be the hardest of all of the 24 hours. Lying back in bed with your head abuzz of so many things that there seems to be no way to sleep at all. Lots of unsettling thoughts whiz around your brain and muddle up into a complicated mess. Wondering this and that as to the possibilities of what may be going on out in the warring country that is related to your soldier. What is happening? How is their day-to-day life? What is he/she thinking? So many jumbled thoughts. Do try to think of all the positive things rather than the negative ones. It is so easy to say but very hard to do. You do need to get your sleep somehow so that many times of trial and error will eventually click as to the way that works best of all. Each person finds that different things that work for one person but doesn't necessarily help another in the same way.

A long laze in the bath can make you sleepy. Take a cuppa or hot drink to bed so that you are all warm inside. Try reading a book or doing crosswords. Reading the mail that you now have stashed under your pillow. Perhaps writing a cheery letter can help. You may find that you will fall asleep by doing these.

If you must think then try to plan something you can do the following day or what you may go out and buy. These should be inexpensive items so that doing it often doesn't break the bank. Think of perhaps a hobby item to occupy your time. Think of getting a specific item. A thing just for you or things you might put in the next parcel you send. The following through on what you decide is very important to complete your aim. It must be a definite thing to do no matter what happens. Something for you to concentrate and focus your mind on.

Write a Diary. Remember it is another day over so that you have got another day closer to r&r or the end of the tour. It could thankfully be the end of a bit of a ropey day that you are glad is now over. This can put things in a better perspective. Think of all the good things that happened that day. Think about what your day was full of or the people you met and the latest gossip.

Playing music softly is a good thing to try. A radio channel you prefer the most is obviously the one to have on. Others find it good to watch the TV and fall asleep watching it as your thoughts dwindle into sleep. Perhaps watching a quiz programme is a good idea and guessing the answers will make you snuggle down until you are thinking, thinking then slowly thinking until the Zzzzzz's come.

A clever thing to do is this: Think of a noun and then see how many other words you can create by putting a word before or after it to make something else.

E.g. if your chosen word is MILK then you may think MILKman, MILKmaid, MILK and honey, MILKing shed, and so on with as many as you can. Keep on thinking hard so that you keep on going and eventually you should fall asleep. You choose a different word each night and do the same with that. It certainly keeps your mind off other things and will have you fall asleep. Try it out and see. This could be a good method for you. You might assume that doing that will keep your brain so active that sleep will never come but you will be wrong in that assumption so try it. It has the opposite effect and you will be in the land of nod before you know it.

It might help you to wear your chaps/ladies t-shirt with his aftershave or cologne on. With the chaps your ladies favourite perfume on. Sounds silly but I have been told it works a treat. A bit of him/her to snuggle up with. You could cuddle a pillow with his/her photo printed on the pillowcase. Your soldier could have a special pair of socks that are silly or sensible that were yours or that you bought specially for him/her. Equally wear ones that were bought for you.

I hope that some of my suggestions are of use and are OK for you. It is so brilliant to find ways to sleep. Going to bed and sleeping is fantastic rather than doing the tossing and turning that does nothing but make you upset. A good sleep helps you to get through the day to come.

If you find sleep isn't within your grasp then maybe you can chat with someone in the same boat as you. By having it mainly happy chat, I know it will make you both feel lighter, brighter and ready to hit the hay. At least you wont have to go through the night feeling alone which is a big bonus.

EATING

When you wake be sure to have a good breakfast to set you up for the day. You need energy to get you through each day. Try to work out a good eating regime because in order to keep stress at bay you have to be at your best. Regular meals will give you the extra strength you need. Do not reduce your intake or you will end up snacking so much through the day and eating rubbishy foods/sweets containing loads of unwanted calories so that you could find you put on a lot of pounds very quickly. Not a welcome state to find yourself in. Any children will soon copy bad eating habits and it is essential that their diet is a healthy one too. You may, without meaning to, try and cut a few corners and get so fed up and low that you just cannot be bothered to cook. Feeling so pessimistic might turn you into an incapable person who loses all interest in sensible and controlled behaviour. It is best to have main routines that you can stick to. Try not to throw them by the wayside. Innumerable pitfalls you can easily fall into at this time. The roller coaster that you are on is bad enough without adding to those battles and you could have difficulties trying to fight the lazy habits. Hunger weakens you. Therefore EAT WELL. Stay healthy. It is a huge aid to be fit in body and mind. You don't want to gain weight by over eating or lose weight due to starving yourself.

DRINKING

Obviously everyone drinks throughout the day as usual but at other times make it give you a maximum type of relaxation. You will find that curling up in an armchair with a cuppa, coffee, hot chocolate, fruit juice etc will become part of your life. It really is soothing. It does give a lot of comfort. Drinking, watching tv and chomping at a snack, biscuits or nibbles is a good time to wrap you into what feels like a hug. It helps you chill out. A hot drink just before you go to bed or take one up to bed with you is good because it helps you to sleep. You could try different types you have never tried before. Drink can be a thing to experiment with which you have never thought of doing. It sounds a rather odd thing to do but it helps if you perhaps find something that you like other than just the normal. There are many types of tea and coffee. Then it's an enjoyable friend.

ALCOHOL

It is a big temptation during this time alone to drink alcohol. A high alcohol intake is not recommended. Some people think that getting drunk will act as a cure-all. They expect every worry will shrink and be much better. It doesn't though. It merely masks your problems for a couple of hours while you are drunk only for you to find that on the next day when you are sober, all your troubles appear to have multiplied. Each balloons from its original size and is harder to handle. A vicious circle. Then it escalates so that each day you drink more as you are over faced with this mountain that seems to be even greater and harsher than you first had. You get to the stage of finding life is hopeless and become jokey to cover this pickle from yourself and others as if your reliance on drink isn't there. It continues on until the state of you by the end of the tour is gross and unladylike. I am not saying don't drink but for you to drink in moderation. Don't let it get out of hand to ridiculous levels. All the time you must do your very best not to add to the troubles dealt to you. There are more than enough for anybody to manage. Do realise that this drinking can easily go wrong.

If you have children they will feel insecure because all of a sudden their parent is getting less reliable at calming them. It's distressing to be without one parent without the other being only half a person for them. They need you in one piece so that they can rely on you without doubts so at any time during the day or night you will not only be a mum but a sanctuary for them. Those bottles or cans you buy to use at home isn't at all clever if temptation rules.

It doesn't help when you go out with friends and they ply you with booze trying to be kindly in the hope it will make you feel better or happier. It might be good to tell your friends from day 1 that this is no solution. I am sure they will understand this if you explain. You are important and so are your children if you have any. You are bound to want to be as right and responsible as much as you can muster. Another part of your learning curve is now known.

Drink normal amounts and you will be fine with everything just right on that score. Moderation is the key.

ARE RELATIONSHIPS GOING DOWN HILL?

All this time apart is dreadful and soul destroying. It tests you both to an unbearable limit. There are going to be many times when things seem to have fallen flat. Many times that you could get to a stage where you might decide the whole process is impossible. The coldness from both of you with less mail and other means of contact isn't the same regularity. When it does happen it tends to be stilted. It can become boring and uninteresting with disagreements and it seems as if you are no longer wanted because you feel neglected. Out come those tissues to make your nose red and top lip sore. Doubts galore. You might even consider ditching your soldier and you have got to the verge of taking on a new partner. Coping with army life is far from clear cut and as simple as you thought it would be. You knew it wouldn't be a piece of cake but this could be just too hellish for you to bear. Things may have been perfect before your soldier went to war but with much pondering you come to the conclusion that being caught up in military life is certainly not for you. This battle at home has come to a crisis point. Big gaps of silence can mean that your soldier needs to concentrate on his/her job. Its no good if he/she doesn't perform the job with the sharpest of wits. He/she needs a clear mind with the fewest distractions as possible. You worry about him/her coming back home safe but how do you think they are feeling inside? They face danger every day wondering if that day is their last. Hour after hour it's buzzing through their heads. They need to blank out home and the love side of things to prevent them getting emotional problems and also they try to protect you from it all. How can there be decent conversation when feelings are too horrific while in deep soldier mode? Try to believe there is a reason to these gaps and moods. They will get back to normal as soon as they can. Take that into consideration always and don't jump in being immediately convinced its because they don't care about you.

Weigh things up. It's human nature after all and temptations can push couples apart from loved ones and you can be drawn towards another person. The stresses don't fit your lifestyle could be a big possibility for this. It all depends on you as to whether or not you can ride this through or whether you can't. Your soldier has little to think about but life at home and doubts will traipse through his mind wondering so many times that perhaps you have found someone else. Don't be shocked by this. They can have low self-esteem as to whether you will want a person that they have now become. He/she can feel like a nobody living in a filthy world. They will have seen many people whose relationships have fallen by the wayside for different reasons and so it worries them that they might be the next on the list. Will they be the next to be jilted? It is only natural to doubt. We are human so to be confused is par for the course.

Be honest with yourself and think this through. It doesn't mean you are a weak person if you can't hack it. You gave it your best shot. Think of it, as being that this type of life just doesn't suit you. This time apart will certainly take its toll. Perhaps these are hiccups with hitches along the way to knock you back often. Problems can be resolved if you try to be as positive with your outlook as you can and encourage happy vibes once again. You will want what is best for you and your partner to manage the ups and downs of the roller coaster and rugby match. However, if things have gone truly sour then such news of a break up is best left until you have discussed it thoroughly & sensibly on the phone or face to face. Hurtful news in message form is very cruel. Unless you can be adult and discuss it with all the reasons as to why its gone flat then how can you judge if the feelings are fair or not. Could it be a knee-jerk reaction during a very touchy time that can be mended and troubles eased? Perhaps there is no chance at all and the rift has shown you both that your partnership is now to be split for sure. It all hangs on to the strength of your love and flexibility that you are going to have to have. Life as a couple might not have worked under any circumstances even if your soldier was at home. This may have drawn out both of your true colours and shown you really what is what. It may even be imagination running riot to make you feel very insecure indeed. Think things as a "whole" very carefully indeed. It takes two to decide. It is never just the fault of a single person. Agreeing to differ and separate might be the right way or gripping on and grabbing yourselves back from this to become the couple as you were before. It isn't a quick thing to do but you can do it if you really want it. Only the two of you can decide and work out the outcome with as little nastiness or rows that have exploded in both your minds only and in all actuality isn't a true fact. I am sure you will sort it out in some way.

A SISTER'S VIEW OF THINGS

Having a sibling away can be very hard. However different problems can creep in at times which need to be handled carefully.

When a sister saw all of her brothers' friends safe and enjoying themselves then great envy and upset crept in to her emotions. How she wished her brother could be doing the same instead of away in such a ghastly dangerous hell. With him being so far from home it became upsetting that he couldn't be amongst them. She knew only too well that he had chosen the army and serving in war zones was part of his job. She admired him for it and she would be proud to watch him climb the ladder of promotion throughout his career.

When he phoned her or instant messengered her it would really make her day and she would be ram jam packed with joy. She was clearly over the moon and leaping about as if it was her birthday. She would be telling everyone that yippee she had chatted with him. There were times she worried herself sick if she could detect for some reason that he was very down or sad.

All soldiers have low times, scary times and times when they need to un-bottle all of this to stay sane. Troubles in letters can often hint of anxiety. Remember they may have been down when writing it and over it by the time he/she has written it.

One evening when she went to the pub she was so mad to see her brothers' girlfriend with another chap. She couldn't believe what she saw. Then night after night she saw the same thing that plainly was evident, these were a twosome. This really hurt her so much. It was the last straw. There was her brother far away and totally naïve to it all. Eventually she wondered if she should tell her brother about it. How would he take it if she told him because she had never butted in before on such things? She didn't want him to come home ignorant about it only to find out by his friends. That could be embarrassing and tough. How would he feel to be the last one to know of this unfortunate event? She didn't want to see him belittled if she didn't say anything. She was split in two over this. Days she spent thinking through all the "fors" and "against". This was no easy task to find the right solution. She had to weigh up whether he could take it while he's living a life of enough troubles without this news to give him. Sometimes decisions are not easy when it comes to delicate situations.

She told him and his initial reaction was that he hit the roof with this news and blamed her for telling him. She felt it was the worst thing she could have done.... Until the next day! He got back to her and apologised for his being nasty to her. He was so grateful that she had been brave enough to let him know the way things were re his girlfriend. He said he would have been broken to bits to come home and be told by his friends. She had saved him from that for sure. She had unveiled the truth and as the saying goes "sometimes you have to be cruel to be kind". She did exactly the right thing for the brother she loved.

At all times in some way we have to become extremely protective of our soldier. We must work out the things we should tell them and any things you shouldn't let them know. The things that are best unsaid. Only you can assess the way your loved one is likely to react to a problem. This weight is on your shoulders. Many times we can feel we are struggling to know exactly what to say and is it fair to hit them with not so good news. Our soldiers are not babies and don't have to be wrapped in cotton wool or for us to try and take all of life's bumps away. They may be living in an unreal world that we cant understand so therefore it is best to give them reality and truth of the normal world. Somehow you will work out the way to handle things because each soldier is different. What one person can accept may be torture to another. Take care and think about it so eventually you will know what is best.

CHILDREN COPING

Children may be small in size but their problem is as big as yours. Their muddled emotions are as hurting to them as much as they are hurting to you. Their struggle is possibly bigger because at least we have more understanding of how and why things happen and that they can't comprehend it all. It's bad enough with us only knowing the small amount that we do but to them they have lost a parent and have no idea where he/she is. The younger ones have no concept of time so all they know is that the next day and then the next they awaken without a mum or dad back at home again. This is why the Chuff Chart can be a big bonus for them to do each night. It tends to give them a bit of an idea of how many pictures/ bubbles or sweets that they have to do. The strange and upside down situation of their life is clearly visible. Therefore you don't have just all your problems to tackle but to be able, at the same time, to help the children tackle theirs.

It is essential that you explain to the little ones that mum or dad is a long way away working and doing his/her job to make the country to where he/she has gone into a better one. Tell them that they will have to be gone a long time because it is a difficult job to do. For the children old enough to know more then be completely truthful. Explain things and don't try to hide what is really happening. They are bound to hear about it from their friends and school friends or see it on the TV. For them ignorance is not bliss. Ignorance of it and hearing it bit-by-bit and jumbled from others can be the most horrid and confusing way to find out. All children are curious so whenever a child asks a question about it then answer them and don't brush it off. Children always know that there is something you won't talk about and then their minds get muddled into wondering why you won't say. They can exaggerate things in their thoughts in the same way you do. Honesty is the best policy. Of course all children are different so you will be the one to judge how they should be told. Children are more resilient than people think they are.

What child isn't going to be saddened by having a parent away? Each will be upset but to different degrees and show it in varied ways. They will be yearning for mum or dad to be back. Attitudes can go completely awry for some. Don't think that because a child never talks about things means that they are getting along ok as they could very well be bottling up emotions and that can be worse. Every day be sure to chat situations through as they crop up. Be open. Talk about mum or dad often. It is important that they realise they are being missed as much as they are missing their parent. Also you must remember that children can sense when you are feeling low and worrying then it rubs off onto them and vice versa. They will pick up both the good and bad vibes. Don't be too surprised by this. It is important to make the good points appear that the bad times are lesser than their minds comprehend.   There can be more tantrums and tears. Tempers will flare and may be seen quite often and seem impossible to handle. All their "not so nice" character traits are enhanced. Anger is very normal. Many restless nights or being unable to sleep at all is a toughie to overcome. Reluctance to go to bed and keeping the light on is a very common one. They may beg to sleep with you. Wetting the bed can happen even if the child has never done this before. Worry brings about lots of unfortunate ways that are extreme. Try to sympathise if you can. Try to understand. Sounds easy to do but it can be so impossible especially with you having your own battle of holding yourself together. It doesn't mean you are not a very good parent by you being unable to solve any or all the things going wrong. Coping can be a mountain that you can't always reduce. A lot depends upon individual children. A great deal can be because of their age too. It might be a little easier for children who are in a military family who live close to the camp and mix among more understanding children with exactly the same strange and complex lifestyle. They are also close to the Families Welfare Officer for visiting when needed and they can take part in joint events that will be arranged sometimes. There is the telephone for others afar.

Write letters as if written by baby and toddlers to their Daddy.

Here is one that I thought was a lovely and special letter sent to a Daddy from his 9-day-old baby daughter Ruby. It has gone into a Baby Book to be read by her when she is older and onwards. I am sure you will agree it is gorgeous.

Hello daddy!

Hope you like the picture Mammy took of me this morning for you! I'm now 9 days old.

I'm getting a very big girl now. My cord fell off this morning when Mammy was changing me, she was very happy to see my belly button.

Big brother Jay has been giving me lots of sloppy kisses. He's lovely to me now.

He hasn't tried to pull my hair again, yet!

Mammy says hello to you and that she loves you, she keeps telling me that you love me and that you'll be home again to see me soon at Christmas with lots of presents from Santa!

Grandma came to see me on Monday, she's lovely, very cuddly and good at changing my smelly nappies!

Mammy's going to take me and Jay for a walk into town today, she registered us both at the doctors yesterday because silly Mammy forgot on Monday!

Think I'll ask Mammy for a nice pink teddy when we're in town, do you think I'll get it???

Big cousin Nicole stayed at our house last night, she didn't want to leave us so Mammy said she could stay the night.

I woke up twice last night, I couldn't help it! I was hungry!!

Jay is telling me I'm silly because he just threw his pillow in my direction, he's a dafty!

Anyways Daddy, Mammy says I have to stop being a clever bugger and be a baby and sleep!

Love you lots Daddy, See you soon

That is something that will mean so much and is a way to involve a baby or toddler to keep your soldier feeling he is really close to home and to all his family.

Here is another from 2yr old Jay to James his step-dad

Hello James!

How are you? It's Jay here!

I've been a good boy, kind of!

Went to Daddy's this weekend, Gran took me to see the big Thomas. I really enjoyed it.

Ruby's grown lots. Her feet fit in her baby grows now and her hands aren't hidden in the sleeves!

Mammy bought me a new dvd at the weekend, I'm watching it now, it's got the wiggles on it and I'm dancing with them. It's really good!

I was telling mammy that I was going to pinch her pegs off the line earlier, she kept telling me they were her pegs and I said they were mine!! Haha!

Oh Bob The Builder is on now, I like that!

Bob is cold, he has a big wooly coat on!

Mammy's been really good, she hasn't smoked much at all this week. I'm really happy with her!

I keep giving Ruby kisses! She's lovely.

Mammy was happy because Ruby slept 1am til 7am last night.

I'm going to sleep lots tonight for Mammy. Ruby wakes me up sometimes so I just play until I want to go back to sleep!

Hope you like the picture of me, I was enjoying a nice drink of juice while Mammy was flashing the camera at me!

Love you lots James,

See you at Christmas with lots of presents!

Jay

xxx

Here are some ideas to help not only the children but also you included. Some of the ways might work. Do things together or have them busy doing things themselves. Keeping their days full gives them less thinking time. Having kids occupied never has to cost a thing. The positive power they give out while at the same time being sure they are able make dad/mum happy when so far away. Don't do some of the things suggested all the time.

Get Dad or Mum to record a tape of them talking happy before they go on tour so they can listen to the voice at any time they want to once he/she has left.

It will help if you get him/her to record the reading of loads of bedtime stories and fairy tales so that they can have a little bit played to them each night.

There is a little talking storybook about a clever little soldier. That can be fun. It also gives them an idea of what is going on in a simplified form. You can get them from Army families Welfare or they can advise you on where to get it.

There are teddy bears with a recording device inside so that a little message by the dad or mum who is leaving can say something sweet or funny. Doing this can be a comfort for the kiddies to cuddle and squeeze teddy and hear it. It is good to have them cuddle it in bed.

When your soldier is away there are facilities for them to do recordings to send home if they didn't do it before they left.

Try writing your own little fun stories or fairytales about anything for you to read to your child. It might be about a toy that always does lots of little things that are done in a funny way and easily and proudly wins at doing anything you want it to do. It makes a child feel that anything is able to do whatever problem he/she has. If its mucking up doing the washing up or hoovering or trying to paint the house and learning how to do it somewhere along the line. You choose what this doll with other toys gets up to together. You decide on the silly accidents that happen when they do them. Any story you conjure up is good therefore don't stick to the same idea and make them as varied as possible.

Doing painting, crayoning and messing with plasticine is something most children enjoy. They can fix the pictures on their bedroom wall or other places round the house to show them off. Get the kids to send some paintings and drawings that they have done to dad or mum. All will be lovely. Getting them is a nice surprise and will bring miles of smiles. It also carries buckets of love and thoughts of the time the child has taken to do it. This will really tug at his/her heartstrings with happiness.

Involve them in choosing parcel items from the shops. Let it be their choice even if you don't think he/she will want it! He/She will love it because it was the kiddies' idea. You could make it into their own little parcel to go inside the usual one. Let them help you to shop for the contents you send. Get them to participate in wrapping the parcel. It will make them happy to be helpful. Going to do ordinary shopping with you can fill up their time.

For children who can write then let them send their own blueys and get their "soldier parent" to send separate ones back for them. It is lovely to see their faces light up when they see a letter has been delivered for them and them alone. It makes them leap about with joy, burst with happiness while they bubble inside and at the same time makes them feel very special.

Go out more with the kids to the park and don't worry about playing around with them even if you do look a bit of a noodle. Get stuck in and both enjoy playing. If the weather is good then take a little picnic. Going out for walks is fun and taking a camera with you makes it a little added extra. It's nice to go out with your friends and their children too. The more the merrier.

Take your children swimming. Even teach them to swim. The exercise is good and it helps them to get to sleep more quickly. Even if they are babies going swimming is ideal. Most swimming baths have times for parents and babies. Go and find out. It is more fun to go with other mums and kids you know too.

Swimming is excellent for asthmatics as it strengthens the lungs and can make attacks less as these may be enhanced from the normal with all this worry. Ask your doctor if it is suitable for your child, as you may feel reticent to go swimming.

Go to the cinema with them or send them off on their own when something is on that they want to see.

Get them to join a group like Cubs, Brownies, Scouts or Guides or other children's clubs. Let them go to Judo lessons. This will get them to meet more kids and be in a focused way within such groups. Such learning is fun. Joining ballet and tap classes is very nice to do. Karate classes or sports activities can boost their morale.

Use games on the computer or encourage them to play any games at all whether with friends or family. Whether inside or out.

See if there is something in a craft shop that can fill up their hours doing it. There are many choices of model making/painting and various kits. Some information of its progressing updates to be written to mum/dad in each bluey.

Let them give you help with cooking. Have them do proper stuff they can be proud of and will love to eat. If they are small give them some pastry to play with and even put it in the oven … eweeee. Grey pastry can look a bit off-putting but it's their success. Have them cut out different shaped biscuits or gingerbread men.

Children love to do gardening so let them have their very own flowerbed. Planting out, weeding and seeing the plants grow is very satisfying. Keep on taking photos of the plants at various stages. Take photos of the kids doing their gardening. Doing window boxes or growing herbs indoors is fun too.

This is a lovely prayer for them to say with you each night before they get into bed. It was given to mums at a welfare briefing and I am sure its sweetness can be a great comfort to you and to the child.

A CHILDRENS PRAYER

DEAR GOD OUR FATHER HEAR OUR PRAYER

KEEP OUR DADDY IN YOUR CARE

WHEN HE'S WORKING FAR AWAY

PLEASE BE WITH HIM EVERY DAY

MAKE HIM STRONG WITHIN HIS HEART

ALL THE TIME THAT WE'RE APART

HELP HIM KNOW OUR LOVE EACH DAY

AND BRING HIM SAFELY HOME WE PRAY

Doing anything with the children or for the children so they can keep busy then I am quite sure you will find many ways to make the time filled and for the child to have an aim. Just like you they need to have "busy time" and the kids can do many things that you do too. Involvement and parental bonding is a very big part of the solution to a lot of boredom and contemplation. The child needs to be reassured. However don't over do or spoil the children by over trying. It won't work and not seem quite as special if you go over the top and do too many things.

SHOULD I GET A PET?

You could be very lonely but don't immediately think that getting a pet will be a right thing to do. Yes its fantastic to have a pet for company. A dog or cat to snuggle up with and talk to can be so lovely but this mustn't be decided without thought. It is best to talk it through with your soldier. Ask him/her as to your idea of getting one. However you must also think if it's fair on a pet. If it's a dog and you are out at work each day then it's not too good to have it shut in the house all alone for hours on end. That is one big consideration. Have you the time to take it for walks? Pets must not be neglected. A cat is more independent and can come and go as it pleases.

Animals are not cheap to keep. Food and vet bills are a big expense. Also what will you do with it when you go on holidays? They live for many years so it's not to be taken lightly. Another thing to take into the reckoning is whether your home and garden is a suitable size. Puppies look cute and small but heavens do they grow so if you do get one think about its adult size. Get a pet to suit the space that you have, should you make the decision of getting one. There are so many things to take into account. They are a huge responsibility. The solution could be getting a hamster, guinea pig or a rabbit because your children want one then think of how it might turn out. It is a brilliant idea but be prepared. Children may promise to always clean out the cage as they look at you with those magnetic smiling eyes. They know they can twist your arm into saying YES lets go and buy one. Reality shows itself after a day or two and you can bet that the novelty of actually carrying out that promise of the cleaning soon wears off and dwindles swiftly. It then is all left for you to do! Then again you can thoroughly enjoy a pet for the children and for yourself. Happiness hopefully will be satisfied. The onus is upon you alone whether or not it is a good plan to get one.

RECIPE FOR MILITARY WIVES

1 ½ Cups of Patience

1lb Adaptability

¾ Cup of Tolerance

tsp. Courage

A dash of Adventure

Combine above ingredients

Add 2 tbs Elbow Grease

Let sit alone for one year

Marinade frequently with Salty Tears

Pour off excess fat

Sprinkle lightly with Money

Knead dough until payday

Season with international Spices

Bake 20 years or until done

Dedicated to Military wives everywhere who waved "Goodbye" more often than not. Who have heated up more dinners than most wives cook. Who have missed more Anniversaries, Birthdays, Christmases and Valentine Days than they should have. Most important of all have welcomed their husbands home GLADLY

R&R DATES AT LAST

R&R is the 2 weeks leave that a soldier who's on a 6-month deployment gets halfway through their tour. If the deployment is less than that then they wont get R&R at all. It stands for Rest and Recuperation. Something desperately needed for both of you.

Now this is the time you could never visualise. Time has dragged its feet for so long now that it seems to have taken forever to arrive. You will usually get given the official dates for it once your soldier has been away for 6 weeks. Hopefully it will be halfway through the tour to break it up just perfectly. How more perfect can it be? The downside is that dates can vary and that position is not then. Then disappointment sticks out its ugly head. Do not be negative have a positive attitude that it will be just right. Fingers crossed you wont have any problems.

Sometimes a date has been given and then all of a sudden out of the blue there is a change of date. This can be a real kick because in your mind the original date is stuck fast. The majority of reasons for a change will probably be due to army necessity in the rota and plans that have occurred officially. Keep in mind that dates can be changed at the drop of a hat with such little warning. No reason to have you worry at all apart from being very annoyed there has been an alteration. It can also be changed or even totally cancelled. It seems so unfair. It may be because of operational situations. Perhaps your soldier cannot be spared if the period of time is particularly harsh. Planes cannot safely leave at such times due to the environmental situations. We don't know half of the reasons but have in the back of your mind this might unfortunately happen. Soldiers have their job to do and they have to do what is required of them. Included in it is this roller coaster that has to be attached to it and it is for us to deal with in the best way that we can. It is all part of the sad plate of problems we have along the way.

My son has been to several war zones over many years and mostly all have been right but a few haven't which is a big shame. Something you have to accept. However we can't predict it. One Christmas the leave was cancelled for most of the soldiers. Tears flowed with massive disappointment and with a lot of anger mixed in. Out came another box of tissues again. One of many used so far. His little girl and fiancé were so looking forward to having him home. His 7-year-old daughter couldn't understand why her daddy wouldn't be able to wrap his arms around her and take her out. Daddy being home was to be so special. The happiness of them opening Christmas presents together was now gone. Then at the last moment he was told he could have 5 days. That's better than none but even so such heartbreak. R&R starts the moment your soldier steps on to the plane to come home until he/she steps back off after the return flight at the end of R&R. So in effect a 2 weeks leave is only 12 days having 2 days of travelling time. Therefore his 5 days meant he was with his daughter and fiancé for just 3 days. Life at home is such a horrific struggle to cope with when your soldier is away but having that R&R messed up makes it a very awesome let down and it digs in deep. It is the battle at home for us all. Swings and roundabouts of emotions. Be brave and smile if you can. Positive thinking and cheesy grins are needed through the maze. It can mean we have to plod on without stopping at the seat in the middle to have a well-deserved breather. We have taken a bottomless bag of pride and love to accompany us en-route so that is a big "comfort friend" to have like an angel on your shoulder. Never forget that every soldier has an identical one that accompanies him/her.

EMOTIONS WHEN THEY ARE DUE TO ARRIVE

The date, the date, the date. At last it seems more countable now. This feeling starts to happen about 3 weeks before that fantastic date. Really planning for sure. Excitement, anxiousness and a lot of scariness. All of them muddled together that you couldn't judge which one is worse. You will get extremely high dancing around with thoughts of that break. Acting rather like a school kid in a sweetie shop. It's a "TIME" thing when you are waiting for it to happen and it still seems to drag. All of your contact with him/her before hand is going to be full of talk of R&R that is due. Other times you may feel angry that it still hasn't arrived so expect some rows too. There is also a lot of thought wondering how relationships will be. Will it be the same? Will it not be as solid as before he/she left. Will the war have changed the situation? Rather scary and anxious. Out come those tissues again. Try to be positive because your love won't have changed. You have managed to cope up until now even if it has been rather a wobbly journey to get there. So smile more than frown and know that you have done extremely well and got to this point then your love must still be as strong as ever or you would have split up by now. Your loved one will be feeling exactly the same way as you. Sometimes that can be forgotten as if it is only you going through this. The same feelings match your soldier and are like an exact copy. No difference at all. Swings and roundabouts. Unbelievable moods. However your up side will outweigh all of the doubts of the down side. Cleaning the house so much will swamp you because he/she mustn't return to a tip ha ha. That's in your mind only as its you they are returning to so they won't be noticing much of the house. But cleaning you will do so that there isn't a spot in any of the rooms that hasn't been done so regularly before. Your house will be the cleanest of the town.

If you are a wife, husband, partner, boyfriend or girlfriend then increased hormone activity will affect you a lot. It has been all of this time without sexual contact. Oh for the chance to be rid of those pent up urges, for a short time at least. That will be high on the agenda.

It can have been so hard at first to get used to that empty bed. The snuggling up and security you gave to each other even with an arm around or the sound of the breathing or snores that you took so much for granted and didn't really notice until you were suddenly alone. That was a very difficult loss. That will be right again so thoughts of that get you onto cloud 9. Normality will return. Your expectations are growing for the time you can ignore the calendar during r&r. Ignore the dashing for mail or listening for the phone to ring. This is heaven on its way.

Everyone will find definitely the top priority is going to be that your soldier is coming home to safety. What a relief that will be to have in the forefront of your mind. Two weeks without any worries for those days. Bliss for you both. You are nearly at that point. How brilliant will that be? It's such a thing to look forward to. Chatter, chatter, and chatter amongst all of your friends and family about this fantastic event that is due. Safety is coming.

PICKING THEM UP AT THE AIRPORT

The day comes. Phew, the one that seemed to take forever. The day you thought was never in your sight. You have done it. The roller coaster has stopped for you to get off. Hooray and yelps of joy. Make sure you have the date and time right. You can't go there at the wrong time….as if you would. Ask your soldier if you can fetch them although 99.9% that you can do. You might find it better if you book a B&B for the night before for convenience and to give you a breather from your journey getting there.

Soldiers are expected to fly into Brize Norton for their allocated 2 weeks R&R from Afghanistan and Iraq.

Although you will be informed of the expected dates of the soldiers return to UK, these details can change at the last minute, or significant delays incurred at very short notice. It is also normal practice for flights to depart Theatre during night hours, and therefore most flights will be expected back into the UK early in the morning. Transport is usually provided back to the Unit. It is suggested this is used wherever possible.

If you wish to collect directly from Brize Norton, you must be aware that you will not be allowed access into Brize Norton more than 2 hours in advance of the aircraft landing under any circumstances. This remains even if the flight is delayed.
In order to gain access into Brize Norton you MUST show an official photographic driving licence or Passport or similar. Plus another that doesn't need a photograph. Failure to produce this ID will result in access being denied. You certainly don't want to be there without throwing

yourselves into each other's arms with unclenching hugs the moment after he/she steps off the plane.

The postcode for Brize Norton is OX18 3LX. There is a small shop and a coffee shop area, but the opening hours are limited. Parking is free. Soldiers should inform you directly of their individual flight numbers, dates and times, and the progress of the flight can be tracked through the Brize Norton Passenger Information Desk on 01993 896050

You may not be going to pick your loved one up so the first time you will see him/her is when he/she walks up the garden path. Either way that moment is just as elating, happy and exciting. No difference there. All of those months apart drop away from your thoughts. Seeing them since the day they left. Wow how's that for an experience. Elation and all other types of similar emotions will flow through you both.

R&R TRULY BEGINS

R&R (Rest and Recuperation) must be done with sensible choices of things to do during this time. Like nothing perhaps!! OK not quite that but a lot of doing nothing is something your soldier hasn't had for ages so that will be precious. You may think dashing about all the time will be great but if you think about it when has he/she had the chance to lie in, chill out and have quiet? You will be stuck like super-glue whether you are any member of the family or friends.

The start of it for a tiny few might be a bit strange for male soldiers because they could spend a lot of time in the pub with their friends for a couple of days. This isn't because they don't care about you. They want to get a lot off their chest of things that isn't suitable for women to hear. Only a minute amount of information is given out on the media and it isn't right to know. Even when they talk to their friends they will be guarded in what they say. Also they love you so much they don't want to discuss the things that probably would hurt you a lot. They want to spare your feelings. It is best if you don't ask them what has happened and leave it unless they come forward to chat about it with you. In their own time that suits them to open up whenever they choose is the right time. They have come home to keep all the horrid stuff out of their minds for the two weeks as they have it constantly as a massive input of it while they are away. They don't want the whole thing dug up by you. Both male and female soldiers will be reticent to go into it. They will be the same towards other family and friends. Try to understand that like you if something goes wrong in your life you prefer not to have the subject stirred up all of the time. Bless them they want to switch off and be normal again. Spend most of your time together just chilling out and doing little, stuffed with lots, as you will find that time flys. It always does when something good is happening in your life. Of course spend a bit of your time going out but this is definitely not the time to dash about to see relatives and friends who are not on your doorstep. The two weeks is too short to be on the go all the time. Your soldier will prefer to sit back with you and watch TV. Chilling out in the home is the reason they are home. To rest and do what they haven't had for ages. Taking things easy. This really is important. Normality and safety without stress is the lovely break they have come back for. Make the most of it.

Obviously with children the leave should revolve around them as to the things you do. This is also a good time for soldier dad or mum to secretly make those tapes of bedtime stories and fairytales or to put a message onto a talking teddy bear. Take some videos to be watched over and over again as a lovely reminder with lots of photos too. These will make you smile and the children so much too, although they sometimes may make you a little tearful.

Whatever you do enjoy, enjoy and enjoy every single minute you have.

R&R IS OVER

Those 2 weeks seems to go so very fast. It is as if it has only been 1 week. You have done some of what you wanted but you wish there could have been much more time of the golden days to do many more things. Deep heartbreak is showing because it is another "Cheerio". Oh dear why does he/she have to return. A nasty thing to confront….that's for sure. Your only comfort is that next time when he/she flies into the UK then his/her deployment will at last be the END of your battle at home which you have gone through. Hooray for that at least.

You have clawed your way through the first half so you can do the second half. The exaggerated emotions will still be the same but perhaps you will cope better this time knowing all the pitfalls that challenged you so much. You will both be able to know the great difficulties for each of you. You will understand each others situation a lot more than previously realised. You then step onto that roller coaster for the sickening ride once more.

Now its get out the tissue box again. This "cheerio" is far from easy. It is the same upset when he/she firstly went off. For some it can be worse this time.

Off you go to Brize Norton airport or wave from the front door. Slow mode has risen up and shows its ugly head. You are back to square 1. The pacing starts again with the staring at the clock as you visualise at what time he/she will be on the plane and at which point of the journey he/she will be at until finally there is the clock-watch to the touch down. The whole mess hits you in the face. Heavens, another mountain but you are going down it rather than up. The seat in the middle of the maze disappears and off you plod to find that final exit. Plodding along, plodding along and plodding along. The worries start as before. Another countdown begins. A huge ache. Each day is one day closer as before and firmly has to be locked into your mind. Another day nearer. Repeat the mantra " NO News is Good news"

THE LAST AND FINAL COUNTDOWN

This will get very exciting starting approximately 3 weeks before coming home. There will be hyper emotions and lots of planning to do. You will think it through many times as you want everything to be perfect with nothing missed out at all. By this time all your life now will revolve around it. Lots of acting so extreme will be with you now. Lots of mood swings both high and low. Those weeks can make you behave a bit like a silly schoolgirl. Chattering it through continually with who ever you are speaking to. You will be asking everyone for their input of ideas. You will still need your box of tissues for tears and happiness as before but firmly stuck in your mind is the togetherness bouncing around in all directions. Yes he/she is so nearly home. Hooray it's a fingers length away. Your calendar will be looking rather tatty by now or the sweet jar is nearly empty. What a visible sight. Emotions constantly course through your veins. It is getting so near to normality that you will fill up to overflowing. Your head will be abuzz. A true pull to add to all the mix of feelings you have been experiencing. You couldn't seem to see that it would ever be there.

You might get some new clothes but nothing too fanciful. Wear the sort of style you normally wear and feel most comfy in. You will probably do a few test runs looking at yourself in every mirror available as you walk from room to room, just to be sure that you look lovely and you may ask your friends of their opinion too. Perhaps little poses to see how you should appear ha ha. I can assure you that these wont come into the equation but it's a female reaction that cannot be resisted. You will know now after all this time how your hair is to be so that's one decision that won't hamper you.

Would it be a nice touch to decorate the house in some way? A few balloons here and there. A couple of "Welcome Home" banners. As much or as little as you want or maybe none at all. Whatever you decide will be just right. Children can get involved with the decorations and for them they will know that mum or dad will be thrilled to bits the moment they step into the house. They will be as happy in every little way.

Getting an iced cake with little welcoming messages on can be good. Perhaps get a little model of a soldier to put on it or a tank. Something appropriate for him/her. Make it into a fun cake to give him/her smiles and laughs. Do it in such a way with the choice of decoration optional. There are many ways to have it but be sure it's as bright as possible. It has to show all the love and excitement of getting him/her back at last to the nest.

The house will be sparkling that there is nothing to really clean but perhaps you will do something as a last decision just in case you missed some job that had never occurred to you before. By now it could be looking more like a show-house.

You will be getting in all his/her favourite food and drink. If you practised your cookery for something new then you can show off to him/her how clever you are.

A SEXY BEDROOM

Make the bedroom all sexy looking with simple things.

Put in coloured light bulbs.

Get some aromatic candles to go around the room.

Aroma sticks.

Put sheer coloured material and drape around the furniture or over the headboard.

Scatter rose petals on the bed.

Special bedding.

No doubt that will be smelling really fresh with you having washed them with a strongly scented conditioner. At last a place to snuggle into without that horrid sand for company.

Do anything that will add a pleasurable touch. You could make the bathroom have aromatic bath liquids and crystals and perhaps some type of candles. You know he/she will be looking forward to a long soak. The first bath for so long will be bliss. The first time they can really get clean. All the things that we think are ordinary and mundane, for our soldier is like a new experience once more. All the things they have been without and have missed are a huge part of their homesickness. So now you have worked your socks off so that the house and you too, are in order. Both are prepared with all your love. A magic wand has now been waved to make this so. What a result to grin at and give yourself a huge pat on the back.

DECOMPRESSION

This time on your soldier's return they have to stop off in Cyprus. They have had a very rough time and this allows them to do things for preparing them for the end of tour emotions. It is a chance for them to be like kids and drink as much as they want without being told off for rowdy behaviour. They need to let off steam. They will have barbeques and other fun. In case you are worried the chaps don't go out of camp to be with other women. Fret not on that score.

They have a very important thing to do during this day and that is to get a bit of counselling and also talk to the Chaplains. They talk with other people to help them. They try to put everything into perspective with regard to stress, anxiety, loss and grief. This is excellent for them to open up anything that may be on their minds. They will be advised very well. However in just one day miracles wont happen.

They could need a lot of support once they are home with much more of this type of assistance. Some could also need analysts to deal with their inner trauma. Life for them has been a hellish torment that can never be forgotten. It will carry through their minds forever. Persuade them to use these facilities available to them if being back is an overwhelming task. He/she could be hesitant because he/she may think this is some sort of weakness that shouldn't need help. It isn't a weakness. It is an illness. If a person has a bodily problem then they go to a doctor. Therefore with suffering from a traumatic illness the sensible decision is for your doctor to choose the appropriate medical person to correct this in order to set such problems right.

Of course you are going to be the best thing since sliced bread but you have to be understanding and cope with such difficulties. You have helped him/her during the tour which has kept him/her reasonably sane. Now is the time to be supportive once he/she is back in your arms. Getting into the swing of things again isn't easy. Other friends and family must be a big part of the support system too. They have to be aware of these possible problems so explain that to them. The soldier could need a lot of space with little pressure. Tempers and outrage are common. Stress might show itself in many forms. Eventually things will straighten out so be patient. You gave him/her various types of cuddles while away. Now is the time to continue it properly once home with great comforting and zest, day after day, to gradually get him/her back on track. It is a difficult situation to solve which might take a long or a short time. It can be a struggle. Most soldiers will return with no, or very few, difficulties. Each soldier needs gentleness and understanding whatever he /she is like upon return.

However, your soldier shouldn't get all the attention because he/she has to be of great comfort to you and be equally understanding to putting you gently back to normality and get you through the stresses and horrible strains which you have had. Both of you have been in different places but you have both had awful battles to face along the way. You have not come out unscathed in this journey. You will have been in an immense and unforgiving duration of the pressured tour. You have to contend with all of that. Take your time. As long as it takes to eventually bring you softly back on your feet again. There is no rush. Don't imagine that you can change immediately like the snap of your fingers. You both have to get your way of doing things back to relaxed mode together. After all, you have endured 6 months of which you hope and pray will not happen to you again. That living hell drops away at last. Now is the time to be of equal comfort to the other. You need to wind down from being an emotionally torn coiled spring and your soldier has to wind down from Soldier Combat Mode coiled spring. You should seek the above medical help as a twosome. It affects you both.

THE TOUR IS OVER. BACK IN THE U.K

The roller coaster has ground to a halt. The drama is over and you can jump off it with all the other people who were on the same ghastly ride. Safely home to the usual way is what you have always been waiting for. The dream will come true for everything to return to the normal lifestyle.

At this point the soldier cannot be collected from Brize Norton. They will be bringing back different types of weapons and other important items and crates. Therefore they have to go back to camp and sort out and take account of this cargo. Your soldier will let you know when he/she is free to leave and when you can pick him/her up from camp. This will be the time you can wow him/her. Equally so wowed if they return home, as most of them do, without being picked up.

Normality and safety will reign once more. At last you can breathe again. It was well worth practising with your hair. It is brilliant to watch his/her eyes as he/she is in awe of the changes and DIY that you have miraculously done to the home. Smiles like a Cheshire Cat from him/her when looking in fascination at your capabilities. No more crossing off the months, weeks, days and hours. You can bin that calendar. You can look at the clock and you will see it has corrected itself so it is working to proper time once more. You wont be dragging your feet. All of your anxiety and hyper emotions are gone. Ecstasy boots that out of the way. No more sending out parcels and blueys. No more being glued to or staring at the phone so that you wont miss a call. No more having the computer on 24/7 (just in case) or checking the Inbox so often. No more dashing downstairs to the letterbox.

All the changes that had to be reversed for his/her leaving can now be reversed back. Life will be fine now. Do take on board that your routine will have changed somewhat while he/she was away even if you don't think it has. Your soldier will notice these things. You too will realise that he/she will have changed like you but it wont take you long to sort yourselves out.

A baby that was left behind may now be weaned or taken its first steps. You won't have noticed these gradual changes but your soldier will be zapped immediately with them all in one go. He/she will have unfortunately missed out on these important landmarks of life. Children blossom fast and may have started school. Their routine was changed too so that their attitudes in how they coped might be different. Appreciate and take these things into consideration. Either way you will all be overjoyed and acting like way out silly clingy idiots. Your jaw will ache with non-stop chattering. Dancing around and probably the phoning up of friends and family with this terrific news is something you will do. He/she is back! Yes you will both be shouting it from the rooftops. This is such an important time for you.

You have got through that hellish journey and come out the other side. Perhaps you deserve a medal for the battle you have fought. After all you were both fighting at that time but in different ways. Be pleased for the way you have got through all of the ups and downs with too many twists and turns that somehow you dealt with along the way. The awesome roller coaster ride that seemed endless. That is all behind you. PHEW.

You succeeded. You succeeded and got there. This immensity of your experience will be stamped into your mind forever.

"WE ALL LIVE UNDER THE SAME SKY BUT WE NOW ARE SEEING THE SAME HORIZON."

THE MEDAL PARADE CEREMONY

This is something that you really should get to if possible. Joy of joys for sure. It happens a week or two after their return. Will you be going to your Soldiers Medal parade? You really must as it makes the soldiers feel so proud they have gone through what they have and done their job very well indeed. They really can see and feel that this country supports them so very much. Doing the long march through the town with hundreds of people lining the streets is amazing. Some will be waving flags as they march through the town and also waved by people inside the stadium. Every soldier must have their heartstrings pulled left right and centre. Then into the stadium or wherever they have the medal ceremony really builds you up with enormous love and pride. You can only enter with a ticket that your soldier will get for you. Don't wear heavy make-up. Ladies that did wear it when I went to my sons' parade had very messy faces from the sniffles, tears and other emotions but not with sadness but happiness and pride. I don't wear much make up so I was ok.

Being presented with their medals I just cannot describe. That's for you to feel within you from your experience. Do not forget to take your camera or video with you. There is a lovely service and the military band is brilliant. There is a Remembrance too for our brave soldiers who gave their lives.

The well-deserved medal for their bravery is presented to our soldiers. That really chokes you up.

They have tanks & other weapons for you to see and touch for real that puts things more into perspective and they also run a video on a huge screen. Participate for sure no matter if it means you have to travel a long distance to be there. Go Go Go!!! The whole family enjoy it no matter what their age. Wrap up like you are going to the arctic because it's pretty cold in some of those stadiums. Any babies must be wrapped up well with a cosy woolly hat on. When I say cold I mean cold and draughty. You then get 2hrs with your soldier afterwards until they have to go off to return to camp. You can buy tea, fruit juice, coffee and sandwiches. There is a DVD to buy and I got one of those.

The enormity of it is a tearjerker for sure. Another tip is to arrive hours in advance to ensure you find a parking space. A thermos flask and snacks are highly recommended for any waiting around in the car or to have instead of buying something.

It is worth every single moment despite the cold. You will regret it if you miss it. It is their day and it is your day. Without a doubt it is a day you both need to enjoy together. A party day full of loads of things. It is awesome.

A POETRY AND PRAYER SECTION COMPOSED AND SENT TO AND FROM LOVED ONES

These are a collection of extremely varied types of poems and prayers. It is obvious the feelings were shown to the soldiers and vice versa. Some have titles and some haven't but I have managed to get so many that flew both ways across the sea winging their way full of love and emotions between each other. Even if you didn't think you liked poetry before I am sure once having read these it possibly could change your mind. It may even encourage you to send some of your own. Sit down and have a go. As you know the rule with everything is "you don't know until you try it"

From Nikki to her Boyfriend Daryl in Afghanistan

A million miles our bodies are parted,
But still our hearts they beat as one.
Over fields and oceans our dreams are carried,
Into each other's slumber.
I smile and joke to hide the tears,
To stop me speaking of my fears,
But yet I worry upon each hour,
Of how much control and power,
We really hold over our lives.
So as I lay here wishing upon each star,
I ask the same thing from afar.
Bring him home safely into my arms,
And please let him come to no harm.
For it would destroy all that I am,
All that I could be, and all that I dream.
Send him love and let it be known,
That I am here and I am his own,
For I could never ask for more,
Than a prince that makes my heart soar,
All my days my heart will sing in carol,
The words as show I love you Daryl.

From Sarah-Jane to all our fallen soldiers

"THE FALLEN HERO:"

They came home tired and wounded
Some haven't come at all
So many of them gave their lives
So their country wouldn't fall
They came from every walk of life
To defend their own land
They left their homes to fight a war
That most do not understand
Each soldier held a loved one close
And said their last Goodbye
From the darkness of the night
They fought back desperate cries
With visions of their own families
Still deep in their eyes
In far away and lonely provinces
They have done the best they could
And the freedom we enjoy today
Has been paid for with their blood
Our gratitude for sacrifice
Will never dim nor fade
And the debt to those who died for us
Can never be repaid
I now pause to remember
How much each soldier has given
Honour love and freedom
So I now whisper a silent prayer
To thank the above for those heroes
And the freedom I and you share

From Leanne to her boyfriend

"I'M STILL THERE WITH YOU"

I'm still there with you in your heart
Don't feel alone I will never part
I am watching you from heaven
Seeing all those things I'm missing
Don't worry I'm safe not lonely
I will protect you my love
Safe from above
With all your love
Talk to me when you need
By your side ill always be
I may be an angel or just a ghost you cannot see
But you are my baby remember it was meant to be
I love you always and will care for you hopelessly
be a good boy because I will watch you endlessly
Just listen to your heart you know that I will be that part
When you need an open ear, I will always be right here
So take care for me my love and in this poem I share my heart
from heaven I watch
From heaven I pray
From heaven I love you
More and more each day

From Leanne to her boyfriend

OCEAN BLUE EYES

When I look into your eyes
I see my angel in disguise
When I feel your soft gentle touch
I feel so safe and alive
You're calm gentle voice
Starts my perfect Monday morning
Your clear blue eyes
Set my mind in motion
Just like the reflection
Of the sun in the ocean

Found by Mandy who thought it is spot on true.

A SOLDIERS GIRL

A soldiers girlfriend, what can I say,
To comfort this woman whose mans gone away
She sits by the phone and wills it to ring
Terrified and excited by the news it may bring
The phone doesn't ring, no cards in the mail
There's no one to help her down this trail
The wives have support on every Post
But where are her friends when she needs them most?
Wonderful advice from those friends who don't know
About loving a man and watching him go:
"Quit all that moping, it can't be that bad
I don't understand how you could be so sad
You have the freedom to do as you choose
So why are you trembling as you watch the news?"
She closes her eyes and fights back the tears
Then takes a deep breath to calm all her fears
He fights for his country and people in need
To free from Oppression and hatred and greed
He fights for their lives yet they can't understand
Why she misses his smile and the touch of his hand
He chose his career, she gave him her heart
To have when together and when they're apart
She had no idea what she'd signed on for
Now she longs for the day that he'll walk through the door
A soldiers Girlfriend, standing tall
A cheerful facade shown to one and all
Shoulders back and head held high
Refusing to let anyone see her cry
She's filled with honour, pride and love
Certain she's blessed from heaven above
She'll find the strength to see her through
For in her heart, her Love is true
She Honours the vows that she may say

Sometime in the future on her wedding day
Til that times comes she'll sit here alone
Patiently waiting right next to the phone
The days do pass and the world still turns
The calendars X'd til her soldier returns
The Government called and took him away
But in her heart is where he will stay
She crawls in to bed and turns out the light
Closes her eyes and Prays he's alright
This woman's Soldier, so far from home

This Soldiers Girlfriend, again sleeps alone

from Leanne to her boyfriend

AWAITING PRAYER

Today is one day
And I have to say
No one has made me happier
So for your safety I pray
While you are away
I don't know what to say
I want you in my arms forever
But for our country you must stay
But I must tell you
I believe with all my heart
That you will emerge
somehow wiser, stronger and more aware
I will always be here waiting for my soldier to appear
With open arms and love thirst tears
Only because I miss you my dear
Stay safe because I wait to hear

From Leanne to her boyfriend

My Soldier
You are my man so much so true
I am the one you'll come home to
This life will pay
As each day I pray
For the safe return
On that wonderful day
I cannot wait to hold you once more
In my arms again
That's when...
I realise that I was made to be
So strong in a way not much can see
But I will cope
And I will pray
Me and you
Together each day
All I know is... I love you

From Natasha to her brother in Iraq

For my brother fighting in Iraq
I think about you all the time
Is there shame in that
I miss you every single day
For you I hope and I pray
As time goes by it feels so slow
Only months but feels like more
Night after Night
I cry myself to sleep
And from you I don't hear a peep
Just to hear your voice
Would help to ease my sleep
The news announces over and over
Yet another soldier down
More soldiers injured and even worse killed
I sit, cry and pray its not you
Each and every single day
No word from you I hear
To let me know what I long to hear
That you're okay
My head tells me not to worry
But my heart does not hear
Tears build up
Soon followed by them crashing around by me
I know we fright
But that's what we do
Doesn't mean I love you less
Its a part of the bonding process
I love you with all my heart
Please stay safe
And I want to hear
Love you Alexander

From Sarah to her Soul-mate Foz

"The Heart Misses the Soul-mate"

I count the hours, I count the days
How much I miss you, I count the ways
I miss your voice, I miss your touch,
And I miss your face, That I love so much
How to describe it, There is no way
I walk around, In a permanent daze
I long to feel, Your warm embrace
And to see that smile, Upon your face
I will not sleep, can't close my eyes
Until you're home with me.
While your miles away, And I'm at home
I think of you.
I miss you so much, to the moon and the stars
And this feeling will go on, until I'm back in your strong arms.

From Nikki to her boyfriend Daryl in Afghanistan

Your my dream I never want to wake from
My heart is yours to keep
Until the day that we can meet
My life is somehow incomplete
You are amazing in all that you do
And I would like to thank you
For you have saved my life my soul
And you have managed to take control
Of all the things I never could
And all the things I never would
I will spend all the days
Living within my dream my hazes
As long as you are part of me
And promise me we will always be.

From Nikki to all of the guys out in Afghanistan.

So brave and tall you stand,
Bringing peace and safety across the lands,
Fighting a war that is not your own,
Unsure of where you are being flown.
Prepared to loose, prepared to suffer,
No other task could ever be tougher.
Yet the heartache of missing home
They never trained you to feel so alone.
But to you all I send my love,
Be safe, be brave and look above
When things are seeming oh so tough.
We share the same air and so I blow
A kiss to you all to let you know
That you are our heroes and bring us pride
So we can put our fears aside.
We owe you more than we will ever know
Your our pride our joy our unsung heroes.

Written feelings for any partner/spouse for their soldier

My heart is aching
I cannot deny.
I'll never be able
To tell you good-bye.

I know it's so silly.
Why do I feel so sad?
Why does the thought of you leaving
Make me feel so bad?

I will miss your arms
That hold me so tight.
I will miss your kisses,
Miss holding you at night.

I will miss your laugh
And the way that you smile.
Even though you are leaving
For a very short while.

You've become a part of my life
Like the sun and the moon.
I depend on you honey.
Please come back to me soon!

Take with you my heart.
Take our memories too
Of the times that we've shared
And know I love you.

To Chris in Iraq, always in my thoughts, mum xx

"GUARDIAN ANGEL"

We stand there and wave and give a big smile
Trying to be strong if only for a while
Our nearest and dearest are off on another tour
Our tears are falling as we slowly close the door
I now sit here everyday writing him a letter
Hoping that the words may help him feel a little better
And then we hear of another hero who has died
And our hearts fill with sorrow and maybe a little pride
So I look up at you our Guardian Angels meek and mild
Please fly down spread your wings and protect my brave brave child
And here's to you my new friends on the net
Who really understand what it's like to care and fret.

Trudi's thoughts for husband Warrick in Basra

BITTER SWEET WISHES

What a price we pay for the love we share
Endless days when you're not there
I entered this life with my eyes wide open
No idea I could feel so broken
I'm tired of existing, I want to be free
Make plans with you – we have places to see
Let's live our lives like we thought we would
Free as birds – we still could

Written by navy g/f Cindy for the Yellow Ribbon Foundation

WEAR A YELLOW RIBBON

Yellow Ribbon
We wear it near our heart
We wear it for our troops
While we are far apart

It's a symbol of our Love
It's a symbol of our Pride
And we'll wear a Yellow Ribbon
Until they're back by our side

So for all of our Armed Forces
Lets Us, that's Me and You
Wear a Yellow Ribbon
For our heroes, Brave and True

By Kenneth of Frontline soldiers viewpoint, Helmand Province June 2008

THE BRITISH SOLDIER'S AFGHANISTAN

Lungs full of dust, feet blistered and torn
Uniforms in shreds but with pride they are worn
Little sleep do we get and our rations are poor
So we ask the Americans and they give us more
Many miles we have trodden in this heat hot as hell
And the horrors that we witness our loved ones we don't tell
In fire fights in compounds hunkered down against a wall
We do our duty with pride and prey that we wont fall.
The GMLRS, Warriors and Vikings have their place here in the fight
We hope in years yet to come they're not our nightmares in the night
But we have our job to do today our orders have come through
Its yet another Helmand compound to be cleared by me and you
No more post again for a week or two no more calls can we make
Till we're back in camp for supplies again and an hours respite we can take
Too frequent now IED's our brothers lost and wounded here where we stand
And no time today to mourn them as we continue the fight in this god forsaken land
So roll on the end of tour when from hell we can depart
And two months home with loved ones that we cannot wait to start
The time will go so quickly when at home again we be
My next op tour Afghan? I will have to wait and see.

From Karen to Geraint in Afghanistan

My darling, I miss you. I live for your letters,
Sweet words you send me while we are apart
I read them so slowly- to make them last longer
But soon they are over and soon YOU depart
For, your letters transport me right to your side, dear
And while I am reading I feel your kind heart
I look o'er your shoulder to what you are writing
And leaving I kiss you, when time to depart
I miss you, my darling, I long to be near you
And say all these things I feel in my heart
I love you, my darling, I want to be near you
I curse every moment we are apart

From Karen to Geraint in Afghanistan

I think of you so often
I love you more each day
I want you to be nearer
But you're so far away
This tour one day will be over
Gone and done and through
But the never-ending loneliness began
When I said Goodbye to you
My thoughts for you are strong my dear
My love I send to you
A love that is eternal
A love that is so true

Astelle's feelings and help for our soldiers

I heard on the news today,
Another soldier killed in action,
My heart cried out "oh not again",
So decided to give something back to them.

After good advice we found a box,
And filled it with some goodies,
We sent it to the weary guys
With our thanks and very best wishes.

I send a prayer to God each day,
To keep them safe from harm,
And to bring them home from that hell hole,
Back into their loved ones arms.

By Bev to Stevo in Afghanistan

"MISSING YOU"

When I say goodbye
Promise me you won't cry
When I hold you close
And I stroke your hair
You must know, how much I care.

Thoughts of you in my head
Lying here, in my bed
I can almost believe you are here
I sense your smell, imagine your touch

Oh my darling, I miss you so much

Poem by Bev Stephenson:

Hour by hour, minute by minute
I can't imagine my life without you in it
Lost lives; distraught wives;
Families having to say their goodbyes

Why we ask, how could this be?
Why has god chosen me?
Here in heaven, where peace is sought
I see you my darling, but can't offer support

Hold onto the memories, don't let them fade
While thinking of me as you grow old,
Remember our story needs to be told
The pain will heal, and you will succumb
With new partners, new friends and good times to come
Goodbye my loved one

From Denise to her o/h

I sit and wait for you to ring
And when you do inside I sing
To hear your voice is such a joy
To know you're safe my soldier boy
With you out there the days pass slow
Without you here I've lost my glow
I wish I could look deep into your eyes
Not full of tears, like when we said our goodbyes
I hold you close in my heart everyday
Keep safe, come home over and over I pray
My life's on hold till your home with me
That day when it comes, I'll sing with glee

Vicky sent to her brother in Afghanistan and his mates

"Unsung Heroes"

Our British troops, they are the best
Standing out, from all the rest.
Walking the streets of Afghanistan
Searching for the Taliban
Never stopping for a pause
Never forgetting this worthy cause
So many lives this war has cost
We'll never forget the one's we've lost
The terrorists are all zeros
But you my friends are all our hero's
One last thing I'd like to say
Which every day we wish and pray
You'll be home soon, war in the past
With your family and friends.
Thank God AT LAST

From Rosemary to her son Matt in Iraq

   "A PRAYER"

As I sit alone in my home
My thoughts travel far away
To the men who are fighting side by side
Praying for another day.

Leaving their loved ones behind
Full of love and concern
Watching, waiting and praying
For their safe return.

Dear Lord hear their prayer
Protect their loved ones with tender care
And when the fighting is over and their end is drawing near
Put your loving arms around them Lord where they will know no fear

From Stevo In Afghanistan to his o/h Bev (in reply after getting an amusing personalised pillowcase from her.) Typical male!

Take care, sleep tight,
Kiss my lovely pillow good night.
Sweet dreams all through the night,
Then wake up and have a sh**e
Down stairs, cup of tea,
Pop to the bog and have a pee.
Out with the dog in the fields,
Feels so good to be free.

From Bev to her o/h Stevo in Afghanistan

As I stare into the night
I toss and turn with all my might
Those endless dreams of losing you
Make me feel depressed and blue
Then I wake and it is dawn
The sun beams down as I yawn
The click of the kettle, the click of the switch
Has the Internet had another hitch?
The screen blinks at me with its sleepy eyes
Knowing awaits a lovely surprise
Its 5 in the morn and you are there
Sending a nudge in your despair
"I'm here," I type as quick as I can
To get my message to my man
Too late the screen screams back at me
D---cs for a cup of tea

From Nikki

DADDY'S POEM

Her hair was up in a ponytail,
Her favourite dress tied with a bow.
Today was Daddy's Day at school,
And she couldn't wait to go.

But her mommy tried to tell her,
That she probably should stay home
Why the kids might not understand,
If she went to school alone.

But she was not afraid;
She knew just what to say.
What to tell her classmates
Of why he wasn't there today.

But still her mother worried,
for her to face this day alone.
And that was why once again,
she tried to keep her daughter home.

But the little girl went to school
Eager to tell them all.
About a dad she never sees
a dad who never calls.

There were daddies along the wall in back,
For everyone to meet.
Children squirming impatiently,
Anxious in their seats

One by one the teacher called
A student from the class

To introduce their daddy,
As seconds slowly passed.
At last the teacher called her name,
Every child turned to stare.
Each of them was searching,
A man who wasn't there.

'Where's her daddy at?'
She heard a boy call out.
'She probably doesn't have one,'
Another student dared to shout.

And from somewhere near the back,
She heard a daddy say,
'Looks like another deadbeat dad,
Too busy to waste his day.'

The words did not offend her,
As she smiled up at her mom
And looked back at the teacher
Who told her to go on.

And with hands behind her back,
Slowly she began to speak.
And out from the mouth of a child,
Came words incredibly unique.

'My Daddy couldn't be here,
Because he lives so far away.
But I know he wishes he could be,
Since this is such a special day.

And though you cannot meet him,
I wanted you to know.
All about my daddy,
And how much he loves me so.

He loved to tell me stories
He taught me to ride my bike.
He surprised me with pink roses,
And taught me to fly a kite.

We used to share fudge sundaes,
And ice cream in a cone.
And though you cannot see him.
I'm not standing here alone.

'Cause my daddy's always with me,
Even though we are apart
I know because he told me,
He'll forever be in my heart'

With that, her little hand reached up,
And lay across her chest
Feeling her own heartbeat,
Beneath her favourite dress

And from somewhere there in the crowd of dads,
Her mother stood in tears.
Proudly watching her daughter,
Who was wise beyond her years.

For she stood up for the love
Of a man not in her life.
Doing what was best for her,
Doing what was right.

And when she dropped her hand back down,
Staring straight into the crowd.
She finished with a voice so soft,
But its message clear and loud.

'I love my daddy very much,
He's my shining star.

And if he could, he'd be here,
But heaven's just too far.

You see he is a Soldier
And died just this past year
When a roadside bomb hit his convoy
And taught Americans to fear.

But sometimes when I close my eyes,
It's like he never went away.'
And then she closed her eyes,
and saw him there that day.

And to her mother's amazement,
She witnessed with surprise.
A room full of daddies and children,
All starting to close their eyes.

Who knows what they saw before them,
Who knows what they felt inside.
Perhaps for merely a second,
They saw him at her side.

'I know you're with me Daddy,'
To the silence she called out.
And what happened next made believers,
Of those once filled with doubt.

Not one in that room could explain it,
For each of their eyes had been closed.
But there on the desk beside her,
Was a fragrant long-stemmed pink rose.

And a child was blessed, if only for a moment,
By the love of her shining star.
And given the gift of believing,
That heaven is never too far.

Take the time...to live and love.
Until eternity.
God bless.

There must be many children in the same boat as this little girl, thanks to our servicemen and their families for the sacrifice they are making to keep our country Free.

PRAYER FOR THE FORCES WIFE.

Give me the greatness of heart to see
The difference between duty & his love for me
Give me the understanding so that I may know
When duty calls him, he must go
Give me a task to do each day
To fill the time when he's away
When he's in a foreign land
Keep him safe in your loving hand
And Lord when duty is in the field
Please protect him & be his shield
And Lord when deployment is so long
Please stay with me & keep me strong

From Nikki for all you ladies and gents that are feeling as though your loved one is a lifetime away here's a poem

" AWAY FROM HOME BUT NOT FROM HEART"

Here you are standing tall,
Showing no emotion at all,
Tears are weakness you always say,
But yet I know each night you pray.
Though you seem a million miles away,
I thank the lord each and every day,
As I can say that although afar,
You are wishing upon the same star,
We share the sky, the moon, the sun
As I wait here for you to come,
I realise that you never left,
Away from home but not from heart,
Right beside me is where you were from the start.

Written by Rachel Louise to her fiancé Gary in Afghanistan

"MY SOLDIER IN AFGHANISTAN"

As the days had drawn near
He said the words I dread to hear
Its time for me to depart
I didn't want to see us apart

When I left him that final day
I couldn't bring myself to come away
The tears I just couldn't stop
My body ached and wanted to drop

The first few weeks were not good
I would break down, wherever I stood
Time passed and I made new friends
Who I'll keep for life when this tour ends

Now am I over halfway there
And with R&R coming up, a lot to prepare
It will pass so quickly and he will soon have gone back
I'll need to focus and get back on track

With only 7 weeks left of the tour
Not much more to endure
My soldier will be back soon
And finally I'll be over the moon

Written by Judith for all of the children
who have a daddy at war

"THE ANGEL PHONE"

As I kneel and softly pray
For my brave Daddy far away
I clasp my hands and bow my head
I close my eyes yet on my bed
Many angels I do see
They're all watching over me
Then they speak and they do say
They're watching Daddy night and day
They wrap their wings around him too
Keeping him safe with his job to do
I need no phone to send my love
My thoughts are flown from heaven above

From Kathy to her husband who smiled when he got it.

"MY LOVE"

It's been a while since I held you close
And it's at night I miss you most.
I smell your scent and see your smile
And it makes me happy for a while.
Then I realise you're not here
And it brings about so many tears
My darling, my soul mate, my one true love,
Hurry back to the ones you love.
 Till we meet again be safe.

Written by Michelle to her husband Kev in Afghanistan

"RnR"

The day approaches, you'll soon be near
I'm so excited you'll soon be here
But within my feelings I'm also scared
What has war and my soldier shared?
Seeing my soldier at the airport
His face shows the battles he has fought
I cry with delight that he's home safe and sound
I hug my soldier, he's looking quite browned
We hold hands in the car on the way to the flat
It feels warm and secure, and we chat and we chat
For me, it almost feels like he's never been away,
But there he is still wearing his beret
The time flys past, it ends before you know
You've just got used to having your hero
When you're back in that car, direction airport
A mission you'll gladly abort
Standing there kissing, your final goodbye
Trying to be strong and trying not to cry
The farewell is brief to save your man
See you break down waving him off to Afghan

Written by Liam based at Helmand in the red desert

THE HELL MANNED BY US

So long these days, they come to pass,
I dream so much to feel my feet on grass
This heat, hot wind, the sand the dust
I pray these days will turn to dusk
Just little things I will to change
A nice cool breeze, a spot of rain
That smile I miss upon her face
Those sky blue eyes so full of grace
I know real soon we'll be together
Just need to bear up with this weather
Its quiet now the wind is blowing
Cast my mind back to a day when snowing
I see my angel standing there
A backdrop of whiteness, her flowing hair
My mind is awaken with a jolt
Back to my reality like a lightening bolt
I pray these days will roll on by
As the sound of a jet rips through the sky
These men and me, we test ourselves
Who else could do this, but no one else
In these conditions we've survived
Thank day by day that we're alive
We inhabit this desert with no one else
And count down the days we're freed from HELL!

From Michelle to her husband Kevin
Afghanistan August 2008

The Waiting Game

Here I am parted, from you yet again,
My Soldier, my husband, my lover & best friend.
Year after year and tour after tour,
I continue to love and appreciate you, still more.

This may sound strange to those that don't know,
Why I choose to wait patiently, each time you go.
The question they ask is, How & why do I wait?
I say " because I love him. What other choice can I make"

Good times & bad times, spent together and apart,
As a soldiers wife I've learned to be strong in my heart.
Many sacrifices have been made over the years,
Missed birthdays & occasions, meant lots of shed tears.

It's often hard, to get through days and nights alone,
But the reunion is so sweet, when you return home.
How lucky we are to have this love & trust,
Even though the separations don't always seem just.

You work so hard darling, I have such pride,
You're always with me in spirit, if not by my side.
I'll always love & support you in every way that I can,
Not just a dedicated soldier, but a wonderful family man.

We've got to keep positive, & got to keep strong,
Keep crossing days off the chuff chart, it won't be long.
Keep safe & Focus your attention on the job to be done,
We love & we miss you, from your wife, two daughters & son.

From God to you all,

    MY OATH TO YOU...

When you are sad.....I will dry your tears.
When you are scared.....I will comfort your fears.
When you are worried......I will give you hope.
When you are confused.....I will help you cope.
And when you are lost....And can't see the light,
I shall be your beacon....Shining ever so bright.
This is my oath......I pledge till the end.
Why you may ask?....Because you're my friend.

Signed: GOD

TO: God.Com
Dear Lord,
 Every single evening
As I'm lying here in bed,
This tiny little Prayer
    Keeps running through my head:
God bless all my family
Wherever they may be,
Keep them warm and safe from harm
For they're so close to me.
And God, there is one more thing
I wish that you could do;
Hope you don't mind me asking,
Please bless my computer too.
Now I know that it's unusual
To Bless a motherboard,
But listen just a second
While I explain it to you, Lord.
You see, that little metal box
Holds more than odds and ends;
Inside those small compartments
Rest so many of my friends.
I know so much about them
By the kindness that they give,
And this little scrap of metal
Takes me in to where they live.

By faith is how I know them
Much the same as you.
We share in what life brings us
And from that our friendships grew.
Please take an extra minute
From your duties up above,
To bless those in my address book
That's filled with so much love.
Wherever else this prayer may reach

To each and every friend,
Bless each e-mail inbox
And each person who hits 'send'.
When you update your Heavenly list
On your own Great CD-ROM,
Bless everyone who says this prayer
Sent up to GOD.Com
Amen

Some of the poems and prayers will have made you love, laugh, cry and open up your eyes and thoughts by seeing the feelings of the others displayed. I am sure a lot will have been relevant to you. I had a super time collecting them all so that like me, you too could read them.

USEFUL LINKS

Below are some helpful links, organisations and services that will probably come in handy and be just what you need. Often you just wonder where to turn when wanting assistance or places of certain interest. It can be very hard and quite a chore to search for these. I also suggest you add any of your own onto it so that you can have them all together. You are aware how easy it is to scatter things in different places only to spend ages looking for that very extra safe place where you have put them and now forgotten exactly where it is! They are so safe that even having searched in every nook and cranny that you still can't seem to lay your hands upon them. They are obviously hiding. Every person knows that feeling. Try to be orderly for simplicity. Keep things together for your own sake. Now smile and feel easier that you just have to turn to the back of this book so that hey presto here they all are.

DEFENCE MEDICAL WELFARE SERVICES

If your soldier is admitted to The Royal College of Defence Medicine at Selly Oak Birmingham or a Military of Defence Hospital Unit, you and your soldier may be supported by the Defence Medical Welfare Services. Contact details may be sought through your UWO or the Army Welfare Service.

UNIT WELFARE OFFICE

Your soldiers' unit welfare office (UWO) is a good first point of contact for any problems. If you don't know who this is ask your soldier or contact Army Welfare Service (AWS) for advice. You can request to be added to your unit welfare office database. They will then send you newsletters and any relevant information packs directly to you.

Telephone 01722 436569

Email: awis@hqland.army.mod.uk

HIVE

HIVE Information centres provide help, information and signposts you to professional agencies. Their core function is to provide information about virtually anything from bus times, employment & local area to confidential welfare signposting. This means although they can't sort out all your problems for you, they can point you in the right direction and give practical assistance.

www.hive.mod.uk

Telephone: 01722 436498 for details of your local Hive.

PASTORAL CARE

The Royal Army Chaplains Dept provides spiritual care and moral guidance to soldiers and their families irrespective of their religion or belief. To contact your local Chaplain or Padre ask at HIVE or AWS

ARMY FAMILIES FEDERATION

The AFF exists to make life better for Forces Families, by raising issues that are causing concerns, with the chain of command. Visit the AFF's website

www.aff.org.uk or Tel: 01980 615525

COMBAT STRESS

Specialises in servicemen and women who suffer from psychiatric disabilities arising from military service.

www.combatstress.org.uk/ tel: 01372 841600

FOR FUNDRAISING PACK fundraising@combatstress.org.uk

Tel: 01372 841616

CONNEXIONS

This organisation supports teenagers 13-19 years and can help with all sorts of problems.

www.connexions-direct.com   Tel: 0808 0013219

HOMESTART

It is a national voluntary organisation that offers support, friendship and practical help to young families under stress in their own homes. Local contact details can be found in the telephone directory.

www.homestart.org.uk   Tel: 0800 0686368

SOLDIERS', SAILORS' and AIRMAN'S FAMILIES ASSOCIATION - FORCES HELP (SSAFA-FH_

A national charity helping serving and ex-service men, women and their families in need. Includes anyone who has served just one paid day in any of the three Armed Forces, including reserves and those that did national service - and their dependants. This provides financial assistance and debt advice but also offers practical support.

Email: info@ssafa.org.uk

www.ssafa.org.uk

Tel: 020 740 38783

British Army Website http://www.army.mod.uk/

Royal Air Force Website http://www.raf.mod.uk/

Royal Navy Website http://www.rncom.mod.uk/

Army Confidential http://www.proud2serve.net/public/viewtopic.php?p=1877&sid=04b9f123719ade3c1908e6e023aa27bc

Mind http://www.mind.org.uk/Information/Booklets/Understanding/Understanding+post-traumatic+stress+disorder.htm

The Royal British Legion http://www.britishlegion.org.uk/

The Brize Norton Passenger Information Desk
Tel. 01993 896050

10, Downing Street
http://www.google.co.uk/search?hl=en&q=10+Downing+st+Prime+minister&btnG=Google+Search&meta=

http://www.number10.gov.uk/communicate/e-petitions

YOUR OWN USEFUL LINKS

Printed in the United Kingdom by
Lightning Source UK Ltd., Milton Keynes
138368UK00001B/208/P